THE
TAARTWORK
pies
COOKBOOK

THE TAARTWORK pies COOKBOOK

GRANDMOTHER'S RECIPE, GRANDDAUGHTER'S REMIX

BRITTANY BENNETT
OWNER OF TAARTWORK PIES

PAGE STREET
PUBLISHING CO.

PAGE STREET
PUBLISHING CO.

Copyright © 2018 Brittany Bennett

First published in 2018 by
Page Street Publishing Co.
27 Congress Street, Suite 105
Salem, MA 01970
www.pagestreetpublishing.com

Distributed by Macmillan, sales in Canada by The Canadian Manda Group.

22 21 20 19 18   1 2 3 4 5

ISBN-13: 978-1-62414-522-3

ISBN-10: 1-62414-522-1

Library of Congress Control Number: 2017957225

Cover and book design by Page Street Publishing Co.

Photography © 2018 by Morgan Ione Yeager

Printed and bound in The United States

FOR OMA. I LIKE YOU FOR ALWAYS.

CONTENTS

INTRODUCTION

It all revolves around love. Cliché, tired, but true. Without it, there wouldn't be pie. I don't know that I would have ever entered the kitchen with a mission to learn.

On a morning that was probably chilly in November—Thanksgiving to be exact—I fumbled down the stairs with a folded piece of printer paper, rolled into the kitchen and roared, "DO WE HAVE ANY SHORTENING?!" Car keys in hand, I was halfway out the door in my pajamas to engage in grocery cart bumper battle—Thanksgiving Morning: Procrastinator Edition—when my Oma raised a question. "What do you need that for, *schaat*?" *Schaat* is a Dutch term for sweet or honey. The hoarse, back of throat, phlegmy pronunciation of it doesn't come off delicately, but nonetheless it is a term of endearment.

"Shortening for pie!!!" I exclaimed, dramatically. I was certain that if I did not whip up this pie, with a recipe I printed from some internet portal of apple pies, I would be the worst Thanksgiving guest to cross my then-boyfriend's family.

Oma, not typically calm, slowly reached into her pocket and pulled out a crumpled piece of paper much smaller than mine. "We have a recipe," she announced. We? As in family? We the family who grew up with a less than impressive spice rack collection? Who ate the same chicken and broccoli and wild rice every night for as long as I can remember? We have a pie recipe?

Taart to be exact. A Dutch specialty. And my Oma, from Amsterdam, taught me all about it. I threw my pie recipe out, hung up the car keys and followed her lead.

What I like about the taart is the simplicity. The lack of ingredients. It is prepared quickly but always constructed with the intent to be devoured by someone you care about. We folded the butter into the flour with our palms, pressing it in like sealing a letter. My Oma constructed it without glancing at her paper, but by memory. Side by side we molded dough into a springform pan and tucked in the spiced apples.

It was welcomed by that first Thanksgiving dessert table and has continued to grace it ever since. That first taart might have disappeared after third helpings, but the love of making it and sharing it developed deeper, from a dough to a cultural identity.

These pies aren't mine. They're my Oma's. And more than that, they belong to the Netherlands, a land that knows breakfast toast is better with chocolate sprinkles on top. This book would not exist without Oma's permission or support. And now these pies are yours too.

The secret of the pie bonded my Oma and I together. She taught the recipe to my mom, and then directly to me too. I'd call her for a reminder of how much of something went into it when baking for friends until the recipe was locked into my heart like the phone number of a first crush.

I wasn't allowed to tell anybody how to make it, even though the dough itself was so simple I figured someone at some point would figure out it was only flour, sugar, butter, salt with an accompanying zing of lemon zest. Simple but essential pillars in any recipe.

It was a fun secret to share with each other, but Oma and I agree; it's time to be more inclusive and invite everyone into our little kitchen.

Round up your family to the table. While one is kneading dough, the other can slice fruit, and another measure spices. Deal slices of apples from the cutting board to each other as you prepare to enjoy the fruits of your labor while working. It's not just about eating, it's about indulging in the time spent together.

Some of the most memorable meals you've had were because of the quality of ingredients. The soil they were grown from, the way they were raised, how it was all prepared. These are all factors that lead to good food. However, let me tell you that love goes a long way in securing the food that lasts five minutes on your plate in your memory forever.

Bake with people you love and for people you love. The best pies are the ones with everyone's imprint on them.

We hope that by sharing this recipe, you share your stories and slices.

HISTORY OF THE APPELTAART

The first record of an appeltaart recipe can be found in a cookbook from 1514. The Royal Academy of Dutch Language and Literature in Gent conserved multiple handwritten editions of *KANTL Gent 15*, a recipe book dating back to 1560. In it, appeltaarts are interchangeable with the fennel taart and you will find no measurements. The recipe suggests "35 or 40 apples according to their size and in each cake put cinnamon, ginger, pepper and sugar to taste." Recipes were written like inspirations for the home chef to build from. (There is more structure in my recipes, though I do encourage you to follow your intuition. I won't be offended if you add in another spice. You also won't be needing 35 to 40 apples for one taart.)

Thankfully it seems as though everyone in Holland understood what to do with this limited information and appeltaarts populated café menus.

Its base is more of a crumb than flake. The taart is typically filled with thick apple slices and spiced with a melody of cinnamon, cloves, nutmeg, ginger, mace and white pepper. The blend gives the apples an edge that lingers on the tongue and begs to be cooled by a spoonful of ice cream or whipped cream, which it is typically served with. The taart is a deep dish, sinking 2½ inches (6 cm) in a springform pan.

INGREDIENTS

It matters what you bake with.

When I went to Italy to learn about sustainability and growing food, the first lesson I scribbled in my notebook was that integrity of ingredients is never compromised for convenience's sake. We'd eat what we had growing in the three gardens.

Before baking these recipes, I encourage a conversation with a farmer. Try a strawberry in season. Then an apple. And then a squash. Try the varieties native to your region and farmers' fields. Learning about the growing seasons and methods helps you make more informed decisions when selecting what pie to bake for tonight's dinner party. Eating what's in season will help intensify the flavor of that ingredient.

Because the crust has so few components, I recommend finding locally milled flour from wheat you can trust wasn't laced with pesticides to help it grow. Make sure you buy unbleached, always. Why would you bleach anything other than your table linens? Purchase butter that's European-style and unsalted, or churn in your own home. If you are lucky enough to reside in California, pick lemons from the citrus trees that cradle your block in an aroma of bliss.

Never sacrifice quality for the sake of convenience, in Italy, at home or anywhere. Ingredients are what make a great baker a better one.

ARROWROOT & TAPIOCA

Thickeners prevent the juices from the fruit from flooding and sogging the pie. Options include cornstarch, flour and starches from roots like tapioca and arrowroot. The thickeners that are predominately used in this book are arrowroot and tapioca starch flours. Tapioca is extracted from the cassava root and is typically favored in desserts because of its sweeter flavor. Arrowroot has a subtler taste that won't have a distinct wheat or grain flavor like cornstarch or all-purpose flour. It goes undetected in the final product while accomplishing an important role.

BUTTER

I always choose unsalted butter when baking and add salt into the dough. When selecting your dairy, scout farms in your area first. The texture will be creamier and give your pie an advantage over others. If you can, churn your own. It doesn't take more than ten minutes and it's an activity that gathers the entire family in the kitchen. Watching water boil might be a bore, but turning cream into butter is magic. And it elevates transparency. Butter doesn't actually appear out of thin air dressed in packaging! You don't need to be working on your own homestead to own a butter churn; companies design them to be smaller than a stand mixer so that even narrow city cooking quarters can store one. A bonus is that when you make your own butter, you're making your own buttermilk as well, which some of these recipes call for.

SPECULAAS SPICE

It's uncommon to find an already mixed blend of speculaas spice occupying space on the spice rack section of your grocery store. Unless you live close to a Dutch specialty store, you'll either have to order the spice online from a trusted source or you can easily make your own. The latter is more personal and allows you to deconstruct what makes the spice so good. (Hint: all the spices.) It's a blend commonly used in Dutch windmill cookies around the holidays. My Oma would tote them back to my mom and aunts when they were kids, and she does the same for her grandchildren now. I await her arrival at the airport so I can whisk her off to the Dutch store where we'll stock up on speculaas brokken and then promptly eliminate half of that stock on the ride home.

Below is a simple recipe for the blend that makes about 1½ tablespoons (6 g) of the spice.

SPECULAAS DUTCH SPICE

2 tsp / 3 g cinnamon

½ tsp cloves

¼ tsp ginger

⅛ tsp cardamom

⅛ tsp nutmeg

⅛ tsp mace

⅛ tsp white pepper

EXTRA FRUIT OR FRUIT JUICES OR CUSTARD

Wait! No! If some slices of fruit didn't fit into the pan, don't just toss them! First, fruit tossed in sweetener and ground spices makes for quite the sophisticated snack. I sometimes purposely toss in an extra apple to ensure a few preview bites while waiting for the pie to bake.

You can reserve liquids from these fruits to use in your overnight oats or to make a simple syrup for cocktails. Boil extra juices from fruits for a thicker syrup to be poured over ice cream. Extra custard from pumpkin pie can be stored in the fridge overnight and used as a replacement for a beaten egg when making French toast the next morning. Get creative to avoid waste.

1

DOUGH

This is a hands-on, intensive pie that asks you to decimate, or at least abandon, any timid nature. Beating around the butter won't do. I'm afraid you'll only be massaging butter into smaller balls of butter and have tangled yourself in a very long, tedious procedure of getting dough. Dig into the bowl the way your heart dives into writing love letters. Act with intention and give it your all.

Start by measuring out the flour.

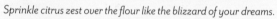

Sprinkle citrus zest over the flour like the blizzard of your dreams.

Don't forget the sugar.

Incorporate together for an even distribution.

Smush and mash the butter into the flour and sugar with passionate fists. Singular ingredients will morph into a unified treat. Use butter that is close to room temperature in the winter. On a humid summer day, use chilled butter; otherwise, the soft butter will make a dough that's harder to work with.

As you knead, digging into the bowl to fold everything together, the dough will first become crumbly. It will come together, forming a neat ball with minimal cracks. My cousin Bettina describes creating this dough as "building a sand castle and then destroying it." When it's done, you should see streaks of butter throughout, like summer highlights.

When pressing the dough into the pie pan, it molds like clay. Press it down, spread it thin (but not too thin, you don't want it to be sheer or see any of the pan) and stretch it across the pan to fill all creases. The ease of working with the dough in this phase and in topping the taart is dependent upon the climate of your kitchen.

Temperature matters. Particularly with the environment in which you're baking and the butter you're using to make the dough.

I have baked plenty of pies in my kitchen without air conditioning or an industrial grade fan, making my baking station feel near 450°F (232°C). When baking in a kitchen with temperatures over 71°F (22°C), the dough becomes tougher to work with, cracking and sweating under the heat of your hand. Though, it's not impossible to handle, and it's certainly an experience, I suggest everyone sweat their way through. A cooler, temperate room keeps the butter firm as it gets worked into the dough and the elasticity remains more intact. Humidity is the enemy, so the chiller the kitchen, the better the pie. Dough will crack under humidity's reign, and sweat and break in the oven.

Oma's dough isn't a traditional, flaky dough typical to American pies. But that's because Oma is Dutch first and Canadian second. The taart dough has a denser texture, much like a shortbread crust or cookie. It doesn't roll out well, so it's meant to be pressed into the baking pan.

It is going to crack. Even if you do everything perfectly, it will a little bit. It won't be perfect, far from a typical definition of the term "perfect." My Oma traditionally rolls logs of dough between her fingers and then out on the countertop until they're similar in length to a garden snake. When she picks it up, delicately, it always crumbles in two. But instead of throwing her hands in the air, she continues with the topping and simply mends them back together on top of the pie. Her casual and no-frills attitude may be credited to her lifelong career as a nurse, and it's one to adopt. The pie will bake and it won't matter what cracked when it's being ravaged with a fork.

(continued)

Get in there.

Use your palms like they're the best kitchen tools you've got.

Your dough is perfect when it forms a seamless ball.

Butter up your pan of choice.

Press this dough into your pan. It's an intimate process.

For the right thickness, roll a piece of dough between your hands and flatten it before placing in the pan.

To build a dough wall, roll the dough into a rope and flatten against the pan's sides.

Finishing touches.

Think outside the lattice. Of course, the traditional topping is a classic choice that's hard to—pardon the pun—top. But there are many more creative avenues to venture down. If a pie is an offering, an edible object to consume and converse and connect over, let it be an exclamation mark on your table.

With cookie cutters or your paring knife penmanship, carve letters and shapes out of dough to get the point across.

When cutting shapes and letters, press the dough down to create a canvas, about ¼-inch (6-mm) thick. Chill the dough for 20 to 25 minutes to help firm it up if your kitchen is too humid.

When your topping is finished, wash over it with egg and a splash of water for it to brown while baking. Sprinkle with sugar and cinnamon.

Perfection is bland here. Let juices overflow and stain the crust.

BAKING TIPS

Blind Baking: After fitting the dough to a pie pan, let it rest in the fridge for at least 2 hours, until firm. Butter a sheet of tin foil and fit it into the pie shell. You can use pie weights to weigh the dough down, but my favorite—and I've found, most effective—tool in deceiving the crust into believing it's baking something so that it holds its form is dry garbanzo beans. Bake it at 350°F (175°C) for 50 minutes, until golden brown. Remove the pie from the oven, let it cool for a hot minute and then remove the tin foil and weights. Put the pie back into the oven for 10 minutes.

Bake all pies in a rack fitted to the middle of your oven and at 350°F (175°C), always. This is a standard temperature for baking. While some pies may require a longer baking time at this temperature, the low and slow technique ensures that everything will be baked evenly and hold the most vibrant flavors of the filling.

Getting that perfectly crisp bottom crust is a matter of choice in pans. There is a variety of pans to bake with—ceramic, Pyrex, tin. Each material conducts heat differently, which affects the dough. One pie with a heavily juiced filling baked in a pan like the Fire King Peach Lustre pan might look pretty, but the pan doesn't function well in crisping the crust. The bottom crust will all together turn into a sloppy glop of a bottom. While delicious and reminiscent of a crumble, this is not ideal for a dessert meant to have a bottom crust. Pyrex glass pans, metal and aluminum foil will give you your best bottom crust.

Use a scale for precision. What you don't want is too much flour and too little butter. You'll end up with a crumbly dough that falls apart very easily. The ideal texture will be smooth with minimal cracks. You can choose to decrease the sugar in the dough to as low as ¼ cup (50 g).

TAART DOUGHS

OMA'S DUTCH TAART DOUGH

YIELDS ONE 9" (23-CM) PIE &
TOPPING

1½ cups / 239 g unbleached all-purpose flour

¾ cups / 157 g granulated sugar

Zest of 1 lemon

Pinch of salt

¾ cups / 176 g, about 1½ sticks, unsalted butter

1 egg

VEGAN DOUGH

YIELDS TWO 9" (23-CM) PIES &
TOPPING

3 cups / 360 g unbleached all-purpose flour

1½ cups / 288 g granulated sugar

1½ cups / 325 g unrefined coconut oil, room temperature

Zest of 1 lemon

Pinch of salt

CHOCOLATE DOUGH

YIELDS ONE 9" (23-CM) PIE

1 cup / 143 g unbleached all-purpose flour

½ cup / 31 g cocoa powder

¼ cup + 1 tbsp / 65 g sugar

Pinch of salt

1 tsp orange zest

¼ cup + 1 tbsp / 75 g unsalted butter

1 egg

To make the dough, combine all the ingredients except the butter, or coconut oil for vegan dough, in a large mixing bowl. Toss until the ingredients are uniform. Add the butter and mix with your hands. Scoop the flour in an upward motion with your fingers formed like claws and clench the mixture, pushing down with your palms to smash and morph the butter. After about 5 to 7 minutes of kneading, the dough should start to come together. Continue until it's in a ball and few crumbs fall off.

To press the dough into the taart pan, break off pieces of the dough and flatten with the palm of your hands. Press the dough into the prepared pie pan and spread it out with your fingers as far as it will stretch without breaking. Continue to do so, morphing together until the sides and bottom are lined in dough.

To make a lattice in the way Oma prepares it, take a handful of dough and roll it into a ball. On a clean work surface, roll the dough into logs. Place one dough log on top of the pie filling, starting in the center and working your way out, forming crisscrosses as you go. If one log breaks, fuse it back together and keep going.

Whisk an egg in a small bowl and add a touch of water. With a pastry brush or your *very clean* fingers, wash the top of the crust with the egg. If you're making vegan dough, you can substitute the egg wash for olive oil or melted coconut oil diluted with a little bit of water.

NOTE: Oma's Dutch Taart Dough easily doubles to make three 9-inch (23-cm) pies or one 9-inch (23-cm) pie with enough dough left over to make a lattice and design for eye-popping embellishment. Instead of using 1½ cups (360 g) of butter (3 sticks) when doubling the recipe, use 1 cup and 6 tablespoons (330 g) (2 sticks and 6 tablespoons).

2

SPRING

We all say in the winter that we wish it were summer, but I think what we all mean to say is that we wish it were spring. Besides looking forward to using a bird's chirp as an alarm clock again, there is the return of juice. Fresh, sweet juice straight from a strawberry. When my sisters and I were kids and asked for dessert, Oma would place a bowl of strawberries in front of us. At first confused by the lack of sugar or chocolate dressing, we'd pause to see if this was a joke, but when my Oma, once a nurse who cared deeply for our vitamin C intake, left it there we dove in. We'd eat them until our cheeks were sticky and sugar seemed unnecessary.

Now when the first quarts of strawberries debut in New York, I stock up and try to stop myself from devouring them all in one sitting, so I get the chance to turn on the oven and create something with those little ruby treasures. Naturally, it's pie that I make. You can't go wrong with a simple strawberry pie that showcases all of its natural talent. But I also enjoy the Vanilla Almond Strawberry Pie (page 29) for the crunch or the saucy chocolate bed the strawberries are perched upon in the Black Bottom Strawberry Pie (page 43). Spring is a time of no sweat and short-sleeve tees and is the introduction to an exciting season of the first fruit pies. You can, of course, substitute the fresh berries springing up in your region with the strawberries I call for in any of these recipes.

VANILLA ALMOND STRAWBERRY PIE WITH CHAMOMILE SYRUP

I will devour anything labeled "vanilla almond," so I knew I had to explore this flavor with a strawberry pie. The almonds are pulsed down to a crumb, which adds a satisfying crunch to the soft, sweet fruit. Adding chamomile syrup furthers the idea of all the bliss in breakfast. It is, as I detailed in a note to self, "SO GOOD."

PREP: 11 MINUTES / ACTIVE: 7 MINUTES / BAKE: 50-55 MINUTES / TOTAL: 1 HOUR 8 MINUTES / MAKES ONE 9"(23-CM) PIE

1½ lbs (about 5 cups) / 450 g fresh strawberries, hulled and halved

1 vanilla seed or 2 tbsp / 30 ml vanilla extract

Pinch of salt

¼ cup / 51 g light brown sugar

½ cup / 83 g whole unsalted, unroasted almonds

3 tbsp / 24 g arrowroot starch flour

CHAMOMILE SYRUP

¼ cup / 50 g organic cane sugar

¼ cup / 59 ml water

1 lemon peel

3 tbsp / 6 g dried chamomile

Preheat the oven to 350°F (175°C).

Prepare Oma's traditional pie dough and your tin (page 25).

In a small bowl, combine the cut strawberries with vanilla, salt and brown sugar.

Using a food processor or powerful blender, pulse the almonds until they're crumbs. If you pulse or process the almonds too furiously, you might end up with almond butter! Add the ground almond crumbs to the strawberries and let macerate for 30 minutes.

Meanwhile, to make the chamomile syrup, combine the sugar and water in a medium saucepan. Stir over medium-high heat with a wooden spoon until the sugar dissolves, about 2 to 3 minutes. Bring the water to a steaming simmer and add the lemon peel and chamomile. Remove from the heat and let steep for 15 minutes. Pour through a fine mesh sieve into a small bowl and allow time to cool, about 8 to 10 minutes.

Slowly pour some excess liquid from the strawberries out. (You can save this liquid in a clean bowl to boil into a syrup of its own to avoid waste later.) Add 3 tablespoons (44 ml) of the syrup to the strawberries and stir in the arrowroot until everything is combined.

Pour the filling into the prepared pie shell, top with a lattice or design of your inspired choice and bake for 50 to 55 minutes. Allow the pie to cool on a rack for at least 2 hours before slicing in!

MANGO CURD TART WITH FRESH MINT AND EDIBLE FLOWERS

This is where winter meets spring. Citrus still circulating, like Meyer lemons and blood orange, welcome the fruit to the warmer months. And today they congregate in the shell of a pie. The custard is silky and tops the crumbly, crusted canvas harmoniously. The citrus flair stands out, making this a rich pie my mom asks for regularly.

PREP: 10 MINUTES / ACTIVE: 22 MINUTES / TOTAL: 32 MINUTES / MAKES ONE 8"(20-CM) TART

1 lb (about 2 cups) / 500 g mango (about 1½ mangoes), cubed

2 tbsp / 29 ml Meyer lemon or blood orange juice

3 eggs

1 egg yolk

¾ tsp lemon zest

¼ cup plus 2 tbsp / 75 g granulated sugar

¼ tsp cardamom

¼ tsp cinnamon

½ tsp vanilla extract

Pinch of salt

4 tbsp / 57 g unsalted butter, cut into pieces

Mint leaves and edible flowers, for garnish

Prepare Oma's traditional pie dough and pre-bake (page 25).

Puree the cubed mango with the lemon juice in a food processor or powerful blender until smooth, about 45 seconds. Whisk the eggs and yolk in a medium mixing bowl and combine with the pureed mango. Stir in the zest, sugar, spices, vanilla and salt.

Pour the mango mixture into a medium saucepan over medium-low heat, whisking constantly to avoid scrambling the eggs. Continue to whisk, letting the filling bubble and thicken for about 12 to 14 minutes. You'll know the bright orange filling has reached ideal thickness when it's able to coat the back of a wooden spoon.

Remove from the heat and stir in the butter until it's melted and makes the filling silky.

Pour the filling into a clean bowl and let set in the fridge for at least 2 hours or overnight.

Pour the set curd into your pre-baked pie shell. Set in the fridge for 1 hour and enjoy!

TIP: When storing overnight, cover with Saran Wrap and make sure to lay it flat over the custard to avoid a skin film developing.

SWEET STRAWBERRY PIE

This straightforward and simple strawberry pie has a sweetness enhanced by dark maple syrup. When something like an in-season strawberry, which I will regard as a natural wonder, is as miraculous as it is, you don't need much more to accentuate its flavor force. Strawberries are the kind of fruit you have access to year-round, no matter your location on the globe, because large commercial farms are pumping them out. We eat them on toast and in cereals, turn them into ice cream and frostings, or pop them in our lunches for a healthy snack. But it isn't until you stroll upon a farm stand in early June that you taste your first one. Their skin is a deep, robust, bright red and the juice from the first bite is the closest to love at first sight your taste buds will ever understand. This pie celebrates the sweetness of the fruit without much added sugar.

PREP: 10 MINUTES / ACTIVE: 2 MINUTES / BAKING: 50–55 MINUTES / TOTAL: 1 HOUR 32 MINUTES / MAKES ONE 9"(23-CM) PIE

1½ lbs (about 5 cups) / 691 g fresh strawberries, hulled and quartered

¼ cup / 62 g light brown sugar

1 tbsp / 14 ml Meyer lemon juice

2 tbsp / 16 g arrowroot starch flour

1 tbsp / 15 ml grade A dark, robust maple syrup

1 vanilla bean, sliced in half and scraped

Preheat the oven to 350°F (175°C).

Prepare Oma's traditional pie dough and your tin (page 25).

Toss the strawberries in the brown sugar. Stir in the lemon juice until all the strawberries are covered and glistening. Let the berries macerate in the bowl for 30 minutes.

Drain any excess liquid and then toss the strawberries in the arrowroot, maple syrup and scraped contents of the vanilla bean. Pour the filling into the prepared pie shell and bake for 50 to 55 minutes, or until golden brown. Resist an early slice and let the pie cool on a rack for at least 2 hours, as it will continue to thicken!

STRAWBERRY GRAPPA PIE

To me, *grappa*, an Italian digestive enjoyed after dinner, is an ode to food waste. Made from the skins discarded from grapes during the wine making process, this alcohol is sipped after dinner. Friends on the farm took buckets on buckets after the grape harvest and cooked them and distilled them in our kitchen until a mere wander into the kitchen for a chat had you wobbling out from inhalation. The alcohol may be strong during the potent process of production, but is faint in this pie. The chestnut honey, which can be found online if you can't find it in stores, is a sweetener native to the Tuscan farm I worked on. This sweet pie is a tribute to all the good things on the farm, around the farm and ultimately, in life.

PREP: 10 MINUTES / ACTIVE: 1 MINUTE / BAKING: 50 MINUTES / TOTAL: 1 HOUR 46 MINUTES / MAKES ONE 9"(23-CM) PIE

1½ lbs (about 5 cups) / 691 g fresh strawberries, hulled and halved

⅓ cup / 78 ml grappa

½ cup / 100 g sugar

1 tbsp / 6 g lemon zest, about 2 small or 1 large lemon

¼ cup / 60 ml chestnut honey

Preheat the oven to 350°F (175°C).

Prepare Oma's traditional pie dough and your tin (page 25).

Combine the strawberries with the grappa, sugar and lemon zest. Let the combination macerate for 45 minutes. Drain out any excess liquid.

Add the honey to the strawberry-grappa mixture and stir in with a wooden spoon until fully incorporated and glistening.

Pour the filling into a prepared pie shell and bake for 50 minutes or until golden brown. Allow the pie to cool on a rack for at least 2 hours before slicing in.

STRAWBERRY-RHUBARB GINGER SPICE PIE

The classic combination is a real peace maker between sweet and sour. If you're not typically a fan of the bite of rhubarb, which is more of a vegetable than fruit, consider strawberries your usher to a new favorite flavor.

PREP: 11 MINUTES / ACTIVE: 1 MINUTE / BAKING: 50–55 MINUTES / TOTAL: 1 HOUR 2 MINUTES / MAKES ONE 9"(23-CM) PIE

1¼ lbs or 1 quart (about 4 cups) / 560 g fresh strawberries, hulled and quartered

2 stalks (about 1 cup) / 122 g rhubarb, chopped into ½" (1-cm) pieces

½ cup / 100 g granulated sugar

¼ cup / 61 g light brown sugar

1 tsp freshly grated ginger

¼ tsp nutmeg

1 tbsp / 14 ml lemon juice

3 tbsp / 24 g arrowroot starch flour

Preheat the oven to 350°F (175°C).

Prepare Oma's traditional pie dough and your tin (page 25).

Combine the strawberries, rhubarb, granulated sugar, brown sugar, grated ginger, nutmeg, lemon juice and arrowroot powder in holy matrimony—I mean, in a mixing bowl—and fold the ingredients together with a wooden spoon until all of the fruit is covered and glistening.

Pour the filling into the prepared pie shell, top and bake for 50 to 55 minutes or until golden brown. Allow the pie to cool for up to 1 hour on a rack before slicing in!

TIP: If you purchase rhubarb stalks with the leaves still on, they may be pretty for a picture but are in fact toxic to human consumption. Cut off, discard and wash the stalks before using.

STRAWBERRY-THYME BALSAMIC PIE WITH RICOTTA WHIP

To add depth to a dish, call upon the herb garden. If you lack a sweet tooth in the peak of strawberry season, the thyme and balsamic of this pie will level the natural sweetness with a savory element. Balsamic and strawberries are as winning of a combination as peanut butter and jelly. Most mornings I wake up thrilled to throw together a toast of ricotta, strawberries, crushed thyme and balsamic drizzle. There's a balance that's as satisfying as it is filling.

PREP: 14 MINUTES / ACTIVE: 4 MINUTES / BAKE: 50 MINUTES / TOTAL: 1 HOUR 45 MINUTES / MAKES ONE 9"(23-CM) PIE

1½ lbs (about 5 cups) / 691 g fresh strawberries, hulled and quartered

¾ cup / 150 g granulated sugar

¼ cup / 62 g light brown sugar

2 tbsp / 29 ml balsamic vinegar

1 tbsp / 14 ml lemon juice

1 tbsp / 6 g lemon zest, about 2 small or 1 large lemon

3 tbsp / 24 g cornstarch

1 tsp thyme, finely chopped

Dash of salt

RICOTTA WHIP

½ cup / 60 g full-fat ricotta

¼ cup / 31 g confectioners' sugar

¾ cup / 177 ml heavy whipping cream

Preheat the oven to 350°F (175°C).

Prepare Oma's traditional pie dough and your tin (page 25).

Combine the strawberries with the granulated sugar, stirring together to cover all the berries. Let the mixture macerate for 30 minutes and then drain out the excess liquid. With a wooden spoon, stir in the light brown sugar, balsamic vinegar, lemon juice, lemon zest, cornstarch, thyme and salt. Let the mixture stand for 5 minutes. With a slotted spoon, transfer the filling into the prepared pie shell and cover with a lattice or design of your desire!

Position on the middle rack of your oven and bake for 50 to 55 minutes, or until the crust is golden brown. The mixture will bubble up and over the lattice, possibly making a mess of your oven. To catch the boiling juice, you can place the pie on a baking sheet. If so, remove the pie from the baking sheet after baking and bake for another 5 to 10 minutes for the bottom crust to brown and cook.

While waiting, prepare your topping. Combine ricotta and confectioners' sugar with a rubber spatula. In the bowl of a stand mixer, whip the heavy cream until stiff peaks form, about 2 to 3 minutes. Fold the heavy cream into the ricotta until uniform.

Allow the pie to cool on a rack for 2 hours. Spread or dollop the whip over the lattice and top with fresh strawberries.

TIP: If you don't have a stand mixer, place a metal mixing bowl and whisk in your freezer for 10 minutes. Once cold, pour in the whipping cream and stir with all your might until stiff peaks form by the force of your biceps.

LEMON CUSTARD PIE WITH HERB BLOOMS

I hope the world gives you an abundance of lemons because there is so much more than lemonade to make. The citrus is a secret weapon when it comes to baking. Its zest revives bland dishes. Its citrus enriches. Everything about the nectar of a lemon is refreshing and everything I crave on a warm day, after a hike or a few minutes after the last bite of a lengthy dinner. This pie is a pillow of citrus cradled in a sweet crust. It doesn't need anything to top it. It just needs to be enjoyed.

PREP: 9 MINUTES / ACTIVE: 7 MINUTES / BAKING: 50 MINUTES / TOTAL: 1 HOUR 6 MINUTES / MAKES ONE 8"(20-CM) PIE

1 cup / 200 g granulated sugar

1 tbsp / 14 g rosemary flowers

1 tsp sage, chopped

1 tbsp / 6 g lemon zest

½ cup / 118 ml whole milk

½ cup / 111 g crème fraîche

½ tsp vanilla extract

¼ cup / 59 ml lemon juice

⅛ tsp salt

2 tbsp / 16 g arrowroot starch flour

3 large eggs

Preheat the oven to 350°F (175°C).

Prepare Oma's traditional pie dough and your tin (page 25).

Pulse the sugar with rosemary flowers, sage and lemon zest in a food processor or powerful blender until all the ingredients are combined and the sugar is fragrant, about 45 seconds.

In a small bowl, whisk together the whole milk, crème fraîche and vanilla until smooth. Slowly incorporate the lemon juice as you continue to whisk. Stir in the rosemary flower–sugar mixture, salt and arrowroot, followed by the eggs one at a time. Whisk all ingredients together until combined, but do not overmix!

Pour the filling into your prepared pie shell and bake for 50 minutes, pulling out right before the center is set. (It should have a little jiggle to it!) Allow the pie to cool completely on a rack, as the custard will continue to set once out of the oven, about 2 to 4 hours.

HONEY LEMON-CHAMOMILE PIE WITH SALTED OATMEAL CRUMBLE

If you can't resist cutting into this pie, like I had a problem with, you will have an oozing honey pie. I wasn't too concerned with the consequence of my impatience and I don't think you will be either. This pie is soft in the center and tastes like it's fit for a queen bee. The salted oatmeal that tops the pie lends a salty crunch that plays well with the lemon.

PREP TIME: 8 MINUTES 30 SECONDS / ACTIVE TIME: 5 MINUTES / BAKE TIME: 60–65 MINUTES / TOTAL TIME: 1 HOUR, 13 MINUTES / MAKES ONE 9"(23-CM) PIE

4 tbsp / 57 g unsalted butter, melted

2 tbsp / 4 g dried chamomile

¾ cup / 177 g wildflower honey

3 tbsp / 37 g granulated sugar

1 oz / 29 ml lemon juice

1 vanilla bean, sliced in half and scraped

3 tbsp / 24 g cornstarch

1 tbsp / 6 g lemon zest, about 2 small or 1 large lemon

½ tsp salt

3 eggs

¼ cup / 59 ml heavy cream

SALTED OATMEAL CRUMBLE

¼ cup / 62 g dark brown sugar

3 tbsp / 37 g granulated sugar

1 cup / 120 g unbleached all-purpose flour

¼ tsp cinnamon

½ tsp salt

½ cup (1 stick) / 115 g unsalted butter, cut into squares

¼ cup + 2 tbsp / 33 g old fashioned oats

Preheat the oven to 350°F (175°C).

Prepare Oma's traditional pie dough and your tin (page 25). Line a rimmed baking sheet with parchment paper.

Melt the butter in a small saucepan over medium heat and then reduce the heat to low. Add the dried chamomile and allow it to steep for 7 to 8 minutes. Strain the chamomile butter through a fine mesh sieve to collect the clumps of soggy chamomile.

In a mixing bowl, combine the chamomile butter with the honey, sugar, lemon juice and scraped contents of the vanilla bean. Whisk in the cornstarch, lemon zest and salt. Whisk in the eggs one at a time, followed by the heavy cream.

Pour into your prepared pie pan and bake for 60 to 65 minutes.

Allow the pie to cool for at least 2 hours on a rack before slicing in.

To make the crumble, combine the sugars together with the flour, cinnamon and salt. Work in the butter with your hands until the bits of butter are the size of peas and all ingredients are clumped together. Mix in the old-fashioned oats with your hands and toss. Spread the crumble onto your prepared baking sheet and bake for 8 to 10 minutes at 350°F (175°C), until golden brown. Let cool before topping the pie.

TIP: If your crust cruises past golden brown towards a darker, almost burnt shade, cover the rim of the pie with a pie shield. You can purchase this product in a home goods store that carries bakeware or create your own by covering the pie with tin foil. Be careful not to touch the foil to the filling to avoid denting the dessert.

ELDERFLOWER STRAWBERRY PIE

What's better than a cocktail? A pie that's fair to eat any hour of the day. This strawberry pie is the dessert reincarnation of spring's blooming cocktail menu.

PREP: 10 MINUTES / ACTIVE: 1 MINUTE / BAKING: 50 MINUTES / TOTAL: 1 HOUR AND 1 MINUTE / MAKES ONE 9"(23-CM) PIE

1½ lbs (about 5 cups) / 691 g fresh strawberries, hulled and halved

¼ cup / 62 g light brown sugar

¼ cup / 62 g granulated sugar

3 tbsp / 44 ml elderflower cordial

1 tsp lemon zest

1 tsp orange zest

3 tbsp / 24 g arrowroot starch flour

Preheat the oven to 350°F (175°C).

Prepare Oma's traditional pie dough and your tin (page 25).

Combine all the ingredients and mix together with a wooden spoon until thoroughly combined and covered. There should be no remaining clumps of the arrowroot starch flour. Pour the filling into a prepared pie shell and bake for 50 minutes, or until the crust is golden brown. Allow to cool for at least 2 hours on a rack to let the filling continue to thicken before slicing in.

BLACK BOTTOM STRAWBERRY PIE

This pie gets messy—all the good kinds of messy—and can be enjoyed in a shallow bowl. The chocolate coating the bottom is saucy, like an upside down sundae. It's creamy and rich with a fruity relief. Enjoy with a scoop of vanilla ice cream for a chilled element that'll take you straight to the glory of your diner-at-midnight days.

PREP: 7 MINUTES / ACTIVE: 9 MINUTES / BAKING: 60 MINUTES / TOTAL: 1 HOUR 46 MINUTES / MAKES ONE 9"(23-CM) PIE

¼ cup / 60 g unsalted butter

½ cup / 75 g bittersweet chocolate (62%), coarsely chopped

2 tbsp / 25 g light brown sugar

3 tbsp / 37 g granulated sugar, divided

¼ cup / 35 g flour

⅛ tsp salt

12 oz (about 2–3 cups) / 337 g strawberries, hulled and quartered

1 tbsp / 14 ml lemon juice

2 tsp / 5 g cinnamon

¼ tsp ground ginger

3 tbsp / 24 g arrowroot starch flour

Preheat the oven to 350°F (175°C).

Prepare Oma's traditional pie dough and your tin (page 25).

In a double boiler or heat-resistant mixing bowl set over an inch (2.5 cm) of boiling water, melt the unsalted butter. Stir in the chopped chocolate with a rubber spatula and mix until smooth. Remove the silky chocolate from the heat and add the brown sugar, 2 tablespoons (25 g) of granulated sugar, flour and salt.

In a separate bowl, toss the strawberries in the lemon juice, remaining sugar, cinnamon, ginger and arrowroot starch flour. Let the mixture macerate for 30 minutes and then drain any excess liquid.

Pour the silky chocolate into your prepared pie shell. It should fill the shell up halfway. Scatter the strawberry filling on top and then top the pie with a lattice or design of your choice. Bake for 1 hour, or until golden brown. Allow the pie to cool on a rack for at least 2 hours to let the filling set and continue to thicken before slicing in.

BEE TART

When I think of spring, I think of the first flowers and with the first blooms, the first buzzes. This buttermilk pie is sweetened with honey and is a bouquet of edible flowers, which add a robust, earthy spice to the creamy texture.

PREP: 5 MINUTES / ACTIVE: 14 MINUTES / BAKING: 65–70 MINUTES / TOTAL: 1 HOUR 30 MINUTES / MAKES ONE 8"(20-CM) TART

1 cup / 236 ml buttermilk

¼ cup / 8 g lavender buds

¾ cup / 150 g granulated sugar

1 tsp cinnamon

¼ tsp nutmeg

⅛ tsp salt

3 tbsp / 24 g arrowroot starch flour

3 eggs

1 tsp vanilla

¼ cup / 59 ml wildflower honey

A handful of edible flowers

Preheat the oven to 350°F (175°C).

Prepare Oma's traditional pie dough and your tin (page 25).

Heat the buttermilk over medium heat in a medium saucepan, and be sure to remove from the heat just before the milk begins to boil. If the milk comes to a boil, I'm afraid you'll be dealing with sad, curdled milk that isn't fit to be used in this recipe.

Steep the lavender in the warm buttermilk for 6 to 8 minutes, stirring occasionally to avoid burning. The buttermilk will adopt the aroma of the buds while remaining tangy.

In a bowl, mix the sugar together with the spices, salt and arrowroot. In a second bowl, stir together the eggs, vanilla and honey. Combine the sugar with the eggs, followed by the lavender buttermilk, a little at a time, stirring constantly as it's added. Mix until fully incorporated.

Pour the custard into your prepared pie shell and adorn with edible flowers. Bake for 65 to 70 minutes, or until the middle is just about set. The center should jiggle a bit! Allow the pie to cool on a rack for up to 2 hours to let the filling set before slicing in.

TIPS: You can use organic roses, borage and calendula as edible flowers to bake in the pie and to garnish with. If you don't have a garden of edible flowers, it's worth seeking out someone who does. I found that the Sweet Earth Company in Pound Ridge, New York, where practices like companion farming are used, grows prime buds.

Avoid spilling the filling all over your oven by placing the pie on a baking sheet. This will help combat a soggy bottom, but do allow the pie to cook for 5 to 10 extra minutes for an evenly cooked and browned bottom.

SAGE BLOOM STRAWBERRY TART

Sage is delicious. You can fry it and decorate the top of risotto dishes with it. You can rub it on your hands and inhale its essence for meditation's sake. You can smear a dried hunk around your house to ward off negative spirits. But my favorite part about it is the eating part. Before there is the sage leaf, there is the bloom. The purple flower is delicate, small and dries quickly. It's not only an ornament to dress pies, it's a soft flavor of spring's new lease on life.

PREP: 11 MINUTES / ACTIVE: 1 MINUTE / BAKING: 50 MINUTES / TOTAL: 1 HOUR 2 MINUTES / MAKES ONE 9"(23-CM) TART

1½ lbs (about 5 cups) / 691 g fresh strawberries, hulled and halved

3 tbsp / 24 g tapioca starch flour

½ cup / 100 g sugar

1 tbsp / 14 ml lemon juice

1 tbsp / 14 g sage bloom, finely chopped, plus more, whole, for garnish

Preheat the oven to 350°F (175°C).

Prepare Oma's traditional pie dough and your tin (page 25).

Combine the strawberries with tapioca starch flour, sugar, lemon juice and sage bloom. Let the mixture macerate for at least 30 minutes and then drain any excess liquid.

Pour the filling into your prepared tart shell and bake for 45 to 50 minutes, or until golden brown. Allow the pie to cool on a rack for 1 hour before slicing in!

SLOW HIBISCUS SUN TEA RHUBARB TART

This is a pie that bites back. The sour vegetables melt in your mouth between the buttery layers of dough and are complemented by a serving of fresh fruit and softened ice cream. It's important to note that sun tea has been recorded to breed bacteria. The directions in this recipe clue in how to avoid bacteria. I have never been affected, but if you're pregnant or have a compromised immune system please be advised that this might not be the right recipe for you.

PREP: 5 MINUTES / ACTIVE: 8 MINUTES / BAKING: 45 MINUTES / TOTAL: 1 HOUR 23 MINUTES / MAKES ONE 8" (20-CM) TART

½ quart / 473 ml purified water

5 bags of hibiscus tea

½ of a lemon, sliced

13.9 oz (about 3 cups) / 394 g rhubarb, cut into ½" (1-cm) pieces

1 cup / 200 g sugar, divided

¾ tsp lemon zest

Prepare Oma's traditional pie dough and your tart pan (page 25).

Fill a sterilized jar with purified water. It's important when making sun tea to avoid bacteria that can often grow in the liquid as it's warmed by the sun. If you're going to use tap water, make sure to boil the water for at least 10 minutes before brewing. Put the tea bags inside the jar with the lemon slices and let it sit outside under the sun for at least 2 hours, until the tea has had time to slowly steep.

Pour the sun tea into a bowl, and stir in the rhubarb, ½ cup (100 g) of sugar and lemon zest. Let the rhubarb bathe in its glory for 15 minutes. Remove the rhubarb with a slotted spoon, lining it up in the prepared tart pan.

In a medium saucepan, pour in 1 cup (240 ml) of sun tea and the remaining ½ cup (100 g) of sugar. Stir until the liquid is brought to a boil and all sugar is completely dissolved. Remove from heat and let cool, 8 to 10 minutes.

Brush the rhubarb with the saucepan mixture, top with lattice or design of your choice and bake for 45 minutes. Serve with fresh strawberries and ice cream. Drizzle any remaining syrup on top!

3

SUMMER

Every summer morning that I can, I rush to the market to gawk at the new berries farmers present on their tables. Blue, black, red, white, orange—a spectrum of opportunity. The lush and vibrant stands overwhelm with possibilities of what to pack into the shell of a crust. In the summer, my family would drive north to the lakes of Canada to visit Oma and my mom's side of the family. We would stop at the produce stands that dotted the highway, and when we were through with our stone fruit, we'd see how far we could chuck our pits into the woods.

There is still nothing quite like biting into a plump peach and letting the juice drip down your chin when you're baking in a kitchen that feels like it's 350°F (175°C) without the oven on. You can find lush peaches in Georgia, but Colorado's Palisade peaches are real heartbreakers. I like baking with peaches that are more on the firm side, as they're a joy to slice and will soften in the oven.

The refreshing forkfuls of pies in this season are endless. The bounty is strong and the picnic invitations are booming. Here are a few pies to bring to the blanket.

BROWN BUTTER ROASTED APRICOT BUTTERMILK PIE

If you're allergic to nuts, brown butter is your answer. It carries the heavenly toasted essence of that pesky allergen without hurting you. Roasting is also my favorite way to summon deeper flavors out of fruit. The sugar that coats the apricot skin lightly transforms into a caramelized glaze, allowing the pie to carry a greater weight than just another chess pie. This is a buzzword pie but it holds its own and you, like me, will find yourself stumbling out of an aroma-induced hypnosis, wondering what happened to half of the damn thing.

PREP: 4 MINUTES / ACTIVE: 14 MINUTES / BAKING: 55–60 MINUTES / TOTAL: 1 HOUR 18 MINUTES / MAKES ONE 9" (23-CM) PIE

10 oz / 301 g (about 3) apricots, pitted and halved

¼ tsp cinnamon

1 tbsp / 12 g dark brown sugar

¼ cup (½ stick) / 55 g unsalted butter

½ cup / 101 g granulated sugar

3 eggs

3 tbsp / 24 g arrowroot starch flour

¾ cups / 177 ml buttermilk

2 tsp / 10 ml vanilla extract

Preheat the oven to 350°F (175°C).

Prepare Oma's traditional pie dough and your tin (page 25).

Fit a rimmed baking sheet with parchment paper and arrange the halved apricots cut side down on the sheet so they don't touch. Smear cinnamon and brown sugar into the skin of the fruit. Bake for 30 minutes, or until they begin to bubble and caramelize.

Meanwhile, brown the butter. Over medium heat, melt the butter in a medium saucepan. When it starts to hiss like an orchestra of angry rattlers, watch closely and swirl the pot around occasionally to prevent burning. The milk solids will begin to turn gold and deepen in hue. Keep cooking until the milk smells like toasted nuts and is brown, 5 to 7 minutes. Let cool.

Process the apricots in a food processor or powerful blender until pureed (yields ½ cup [118 ml] of puree). Let cool.

Mix the sugar, eggs and arrowroot starch flour together. Stir the apricot puree into the buttermilk and vanilla, then pour it in a slow, steady stream into the sugar mixture. Finally, whisk in the browned butter and pour into your prepared pie shell.

Bake for 55 to 60 minutes, or until the center of the pie is just set. There should be a bit of a jiggle in the center of your pie. Allow the pie to cool and continue to set for at least 2 hours before slicing in.

ROSE HIP AND POACHED CHERRY PIE WITH PISTACHIO CRUMBLE

Lush rose gardens scream summer to me. Growing up in the country, friends who had the pools we took up a residency in typically also had accompanying rose gardens. Combine the hypnotic scent with the essential poolside snacking of sweet cherries and indulge in this pie before school starts. The pie thickens nicely as it bakes.

PREP: 19 MINUTES / ACTIVE: 6 MINUTES / BAKING: 50-55 MINUTES / TOTAL: 1 HOUR 35 MINUTES / MAKES ONE 9"(23-CM) PIE

¼ cup / 59 ml water

¼ cup / 62 g sugar

4 dried rose hip tea bags

1½ lbs (about 5 cups) / 678 g cherries, pitted

3 tbsp / 24 g tapioca starch flour

1 tsp vanilla extract

Ice cream, for serving, optional

Rose syrup, for serving, optional

PISTACHIO-SPECULAAS CRUMBLE

1 cup / 120 g unbleached all-purpose flour

¼ cup / 50 g maple sugar

⅛ tsp salt

½ tsp Speculaas Spice (page 16)

½ cup (1 stick) / 115 g unsalted butter, cut into cubes

¼ cup / 40 g raw pistachios

¼ cup / 22 g old fashioned oats

Preheat the oven to 350°F (175°C).

Prepare Oma's traditional pie dough and your tin (page 25).

Combine the water and sugar in a medium saucepan, stirring occasionally over medium heat until the sugar is dissolved. Do not bring to a boil! Reduce the heat to low and steep the rose hip in the syrup for 10 minutes, until fragrant. Add the pitted cherries, tossing with a wooden spoon to cover all with liquid and steep, stirring occasionally. The cherries should break and release their juices, 11 to 15 minutes. Transfer the cherries to a mixing bowl using a slotted spoon. Let them cool for up to 20 minutes. Reserve the simple syrup you made by pouring the liquid from the saucepan through a fine mesh sieve into a sterilized mason jar for later use.

Combine the poached cherries with the tapioca starch flour and vanilla. Pour the filling into your prepared pie shell.

To make the crumble, combine flour, maple sugar, salt and speculaas together until unified. Add squares of butter and press flat into petals. Mix using your fingertips until the butter is worked into the flour and varies in sizes from peas to quarters. Toss in the pistachios and oats and ornament the top of the filling with the crumble.

Bake for 50 to 55 minutes until golden brown. Allow the pie to cool on a rack for up to 2 hours, letting the filling continue to thicken.

Serve with ice cream and rose syrup, if you choose.

MIXED BERRY CHOCOLATE SURPRISE PIE

It's your basic berry pie, with a simple, rich addition. I call it a surprise because every forkful beckons a unique bite. The three varieties of berries blast a combination of sweet, tart and sour flavors at the tip of your fork. This pie can only be made better by substituting any of the below berries with those native to your region, be that marionberries or boysenberries.

PREP: 4 MINUTES / ACTIVE: 2 MINUTES / BAKING: 50 MINUTES / TOTAL: 56 MINUTES / MAKES ONE 9"(23-CM) PIE

1 cup / 143 g blueberries

1 cup / 134 g raspberries

1 cup / 140 g blackberries

1 tbsp / 14 ml lemon juice

1 tsp lemon zest

¼ cup / 54 g granulated sugar

¼ cup / 54 g light brown sugar

3 tbsp / 24 g arrowroot starch flour

¼ cup + 2 tbsp / 54 g chopped dark chocolate (71%)

Preheat the oven to 350°F (175°C).

Prepare Oma's traditional pie dough and your tin (page 25).

Combine the berries in a medium mixing bowl and cover with lemon juice.

In a separate bowl, use the force of your fingers to massage the lemon zest into the sugar and brown sugar to release its oil and essentially the power of zest. Add the arrowroot starch flour and stir to fully incorporate. You shouldn't see any remaining clumps of the arrowroot flour.

Mix the lemon sugar into the berries, followed by the chopped chocolate, until everything is evenly distributed.

Pour the filling into your prepared pie shell and bake for 50 to 55 minutes, or until golden brown.

CLASSIC BLUEBERRY PIE

Even if you don't enjoy blueberries straight from the pint, the fruit baked into muffins, pancakes and pies have a place in the dessert world. These tart little balls are a versatile bunch. Each pint can carry an array of sour and sweet. It's everything manufactured candy wishes it could be.

PREP: 4 MINUTES / ACTIVE: 1 MINUTE / BAKING: 45–50 MINUTES / TOTAL: 50 TO 55 MINUTES / MAKES ONE 9"(23-CM) PIE

1 lb (about 3¼ cups) / 450 g fresh blueberries

2 tbsp / 29 ml freshly squeezed orange juice

1 tsp orange zest

½ cup / 100 g granulated sugar

2 tbsp / 29 ml honey

¼ cup / 33 g tapioca flour

Preheat the oven to 350°F (175°C).

Prepare Oma's traditional pie dough and your tin (page 25).

Mix all the ingredients together and pour into your prepared pie shell, topping with a lattice or inspired design.

Bake the pie for 45 to 50 minutes, or until the filling is bubbling and the crust is golden. Allow the pie to cool on a rack for at least 2 hours before slicing in.

ROBUST PEACH-RASPBERRY PIE WITH CORNFLAKE CRUMBLE

The beautiful thing about food is that it beckons memories and because of that, you get a better glimpse into a person's world. Which is what inspired this pie. My dad shared with me that, as a kid in Virginia, he'd race home after school to fix a bowl of cornflakes with peaches in it and "a lot of sugar...a LOT of sugar." It's something I would never know because I hadn't ever asked what he ate for breakfast as a kid but this afterschool snack was once the beacon of my dad's day and I wanted to recreate that excitement with this pie.

Peach and raspberry are a winning combination, and the cornflake crumble on top strikes the sentimental element with a good crunch.

PREP: 11 MINUTES / ACTIVE: 3 MINUTES / BAKING: 50–55 MINUTES / TOTAL: 1 HOUR 4 MINUTES / MAKES TWO 8" (20-CM) PIES OR ONE 10" (25-CM) PIE

1 lb 4 oz (about 3 large) / 562 g peaches, sliced ¼" (6-mm) thick

11 oz (about 2½ cups) / 318 g raspberries, divided

¼ cup / 59 ml dark maple syrup

¼ tsp vanilla extract

3 tbsp / 24 g tapioca starch flour

½ tsp cinnamon

2 tbsp / 18 g light brown sugar

CORNFLAKE CRUMBLE

1 cup / 120 g unbleached all-purpose flour

2 tbsp / 25 g granulated sugar

½ tsp cinnamon

Pinch of salt

½ cup (1 stick) / 115 g unsalted butter, cut into cubes

¾ cups / 20 g smashed cornflakes

Preheat the oven to 350°F (175°C).

Prepare Oma's traditional pie dough and your tin (page 25).

Combine the peach slices with 2 cups (255 g) of raspberries in a large mixing bowl.

In a small mixing bowl, mash the remaining ½ cup (63 g) of raspberries with the back of a fork. Stir in the maple syrup, vanilla, tapioca starch flour and cinnamon until fully incorporated. Stir in the brown sugar.

Pour the mashed raspberry mixture over the peaches and raspberries, mixing together with a wooden spoon until all the fruit is covered and glistening. Transfer the filling to your prepared pie shell.

To make the crumble, combine the flour, sugar, cinnamon and salt together until unified. Add the squares of butter and press flat into petals. Mix using your fingertips until the butter is worked into the flour and varies in sizes from peas to quarters. Toss in the cornflakes and ornament the top of the filling with the crumble.

Bake for 50 to 55 minutes, or until golden brown. Allow the pie to cool on a rack for at least 1 hour before slicing in.

TIP: When picking peaches to bake, I go for those that are on the cusp of ripeness. The firm fruit is a pleasure to work with (when slicing), bakes well and maintains the juicy sweetness of what would be its future ripe self.

Leave the skin on, after a good wash, to reduce food waste. The slices will be thin enough to go under the radar.

LEMON ZEST DARK BERRY PIE

Baking berry pies is as straightforward as buttering toast. Because berries don't require a peel, it's the kind of dessert you can throw together in a tight timeframe. This pie brings the tart bite of dark berries with an unexpected refresher in the form of chopped mint. Lemon zest elevates all flavors and adds its own citrus delight to the party. When looking for the right berries, roam country roads and stroll through woods foraging for wild, edible ones to use for the ultimate local and natural dessert. Beware of bears though; if you don't cross them on the foraging journey, they might come knocking when the aroma of baked berries wafts their way.

PREP: 6 MINUTES / ACTIVE: 2 MINUTES / BAKING: 45–50 MINUTES / TOTAL: 58 MINUTES / MAKES ONE 9"(23-CM) PIE

¼ cup / 54 g light brown sugar

Zest of 2 small lemons

9.9 oz (about 2 cups) / 282 g blueberries

12.8 oz (about 3 cups) / 362 g blackberries

2 tbsp / 29 ml lemon juice

3 mint leaves, minced

¼ cup / 33 g arrowroot starch flour

Preheat the oven to 350°F (175°C).

Prepare Oma's traditional pie dough and your tin (page 25).

Crush the brown sugar with the back of a spoon on the bottom of a mixing bowl. Mix in the zest with your fingertips until it's a little wet. Pour the berries over the zesty sugar, followed by the lemon juice, mint and arrowroot starch flour. Toss together and let the berries macerate for 30 minutes.

Drain any excess liquid, pour the sugared berries into your prepared pie shell and top with a lattice or inspired design. Bake for 50 minutes, or until golden brown. Allow the pie to cool on a rack for at least 2 hours.

MOLASSES, PEACH AND CANDIED GINGER PIE

Gingerbread is one of the first cakes I baked from scratch. It's when I learned that molasses and ginger are a harmonic pairing that can be enjoyed separately, but are a power couple when together. Thus, cake inspires pie, breaking through dessert barriers. Enjoy this pie with a refreshing scoop of vanilla ice cream on top to play against the internal heat.

PREP: 14 MINUTES / ACTIVE: 2 MINUTES / BAKING: 50 MINUTES / TOTAL: 1 HOUR 6 MINUTES / MAKES ONE 9"(23-CM) PIE

1½ lbs (about 4–5 large) / 764 g peaches, sliced ¼" (6-mm) thick

2 tbsp / 30 g crystallized ginger, chopped

2 tbsp / 30 ml molasses

1 tbsp / 14 ml honey

1 tbsp / 12 g dark brown sugar

2 tbsp / 29 ml lemon juice

3 tbsp / 24 g unbleached all-purpose flour

¼ tsp nutmeg

½ tsp cinnamon

Pinch of salt

Preheat the oven to 350°F (175°C).

Prepare Oma's traditional pie dough and your tin (page 25).

Add all the ingredients to a large bowl. Stir with a wooden spoon to combine all the ingredients together until the peaches are fully covered and glistening under the kitchen lights.

Bake for 50 minutes, or until golden brown. Allow the pie to cool for at least 2 hours on a rack before slicing in!

CHILI CHERRY PIE WITH CHOCOLATE CRUMBLE

This isn't the kind of pie to make in a hurry. Whenever pitting cherries is involved, it's best to wrap yourself in some protective cloth, settle into the counter and have a friend, family member or great playlist nearby. Some of the best conversations and revelations have come when my hands were sticky with juice and dyed red. It's more of a meditation than a menial task, and the time spent doing it should be appreciated. The mindfulness present in making this pie will not only be evident in the pie itself once served, but also most likely in your life too. We should all pit more cherries. Sweet cherries against the heat of chili confuses your taste buds in a subtle but exciting way and takes care of two cravings at once.

PREP: 20 MINUTES / ACTIVE: 2 MINUTES / BAKING: 55–60 MINUTES / TOTAL: 1 HOUR 22 MINUTES / MAKES ONE 9"(23-CM) PIE

1½ lbs (about 5 cups) / 678 g sweet cherries, pitted

2 tbsp / 29 ml lemon juice

1 tsp lemon zest

1 tsp chili pepper, finely minced, or ⅛ tsp ground cayenne pepper

¼ cup / 33 g tapioca starch flour

¼ cup / 56 g granulated sugar

¼ tsp salt

CHOCOLATE CRUMBLE

1 cup / 120 g unbleached, all-purpose flour

1 tbsp / 7 g cocoa powder

2 tbsp / 25 g light brown sugar

⅛ tsp salt

½ cup (1 stick) / 115 g unsalted butter, cut into cubes

⅓ cup / 60 g dark chocolate, coarsely chopped

Preheat the oven to 350°F (175°C).

Prepare Oma's traditional pie dough and your tin (page 25).

Combine the cherries, lemon juice, lemon zest, chili pepper, tapioca flour, sugar and salt with a wooden spoon until all the cherries are covered and glistening with sugar like miniature disco balls. There should be no remaining lumps of tapioca starch flour.

To make the chocolate crumble, combine the flour, cocoa powder, brown sugar and salt together until unified. Add the squares of butter and press flat into petals. Mix together using your fingertips until the butter is worked into the flour and varies in sizes from peas to quarters. Toss in chopped chocolate and ornament the top of the cherries with the crumble.

Bake for 55 to 60 minutes. Allow the pie to cool on a rack for at least 2 hours before slicing in!

ZESTY PEACH PIE WITH ALMOND CRUMBLE

Zest makes everything just a little bit better. The added element forces other flavors to stand out. Suddenly the peach is sweeter against its tang. This dessert captures summer in a pie shell. Like sipping lemonade and snacking on peaches under a striped umbrella on a beach day, with a consistent and cooling sea breeze.

PREP: 11 MINUTES / ACTIVE: 3 MINUTES / BAKING: 55 MINUTES / TOTAL: 1 HOUR 9 MINUTES / MAKES ONE 10" (25-CM) PIE

2 lbs (about 5 large peaches) / 895 g peaches, sliced ¼" (6-mm) thick

1 tbsp / 14 ml lemon juice

1 tbsp / 6 g orange zest

¼ cup / 50 g granulated sugar

3 tbsp / 24 g unbleached all-purpose flour

½ tsp cinnamon

¼ tsp ginger

¼ tsp nutmeg

⅛ tsp salt

ALMOND CRUMBLE

1 cup / 120 g unbleached all-purpose flour

2 tbsp / 25 g dark brown sugar

1 tsp cinnamon

¼ tsp salt

6 tbsp / 85 g unsalted butter, cut into squares

¼ cup / 35 g raw almonds, coarsely chopped

Preheat the oven to 350°F (175°C).

Prepare Oma's traditional pie dough and your tin (page 25).

In a large bowl, mix the sliced peaches with the lemon juice. In a small bowl, massage the orange zest into the sugar until it's slightly wet. Stir the sugar into the peaches, followed by the flour, cinnamon, ginger, nutmeg and salt.

To make the almond crumble, combine the flour, brown sugar, cinnamon and salt together until unified. Add the squares of butter and press flat into petals. Mix using your fingertips until the butter is worked into the flour and varies in sizes from peas to quarters. Toss in the chopped almonds and ornament the top of the peaches with the crumble.

Bake for 55 minutes until the crust is golden brown and your kitchen is engulfed in a sweet scent. Allow the pie to cool on a rack for at least 1 hour before slicing in.

HONEY APRICOT OPEN-FACED TART

Celebrate the apricot with a tart that accentuates its natural wonder with another natural wonder—honey. A stroll through the farmers market in summer will greet you with mountains of stone fruit. You'll want to conquer each peak. I believe that you can do that especially when there are pies like this one to bake.

PREP: 7 MINUTES / ACTIVE: 3 MINUTES / BAKING: 45 MINUTES / TOTAL: 55 MINUTES / MAKES ONE 9" (23-CM) TART

1 lb 4 oz (about 6 apricots) / 614 g apricots, halved and pitted

¼ cup / 50 ml honey

1 tbsp / 12 g dark brown sugar

3 tbsp / 24 g arrowroot starch flour

½ tsp cinnamon

¼ tsp ginger

1 tsp lemon zest

⅛ tsp salt

Preheat the oven to 350°F (175°C).

Prepare Oma's traditional pie dough and your tin (page 25).

Combine all the ingredients in a mixing bowl with a wooden spoon, making sure that the apricots are completely covered and glistening under the kitchen lights. Make sure to scrape out all the honey from your measuring cup with a rubber spatula. Pour the filling in your prepared pie shell.

Bake for 45 to 50 minutes, or until golden brown. Allow the pie to cool on a rack for up to 1 hour. Enjoy topped with whipped cream!

TIP: To avoid food waste, don't peel the apricots. The skins are perfectly edible.

STONE FRUIT MEDLEY PIE

Stone fruits are the song of summer. Apricots, plums, peaches and nectarines ornament farmers market stands. These little globes of juice pack flavor and, together in a pie shell, bake into an edible sort of fruit punch.

PREP: 10 MINUTES / ACTIVE: 2 MINUTES / BAKING: 50 MINUTES / TOTAL: 1 HOUR 2 MINUTES / MAKES ONE 10"(25-CM) PIE

13 oz (about 2 large) / 368 g peaches, sliced ¼" (6-mm) thick

6 oz (about 2 small) / 169 g apricots, pitted and sliced

8 oz (about 2 small) / 251 g plums, pitted and sliced

½ cup / 100 g light brown sugar

¼ cup / 33 g tapioca starch flour

¼ tsp ground ginger

⅛ tsp ground cinnamon

1 tbsp / 15 g lemon verbena, finely chopped

1 tbsp / 15 ml lemon juice

Preheat the oven to 350°F (175°C).

Prepare Oma's traditional pie dough and your tin (page 25).

Combine the peaches, apricots, plums, brown sugar, tapioca starch flour, ginger, cinnamon, lemon verbena and lemon juice in a mixing bowl. Mix until all the fruit is covered and glistening under the kitchen lights. There should be no lumps of tapioca starch flour found in the mixture.

Pour the filling into your prepared pie shell and bake for 50 minutes. Allow the pie to cool on a rack for at least 2 hours before slicing in.

> TIP: You can use yellow or white peaches here or substitute peaches with white nectarines, which tend to be very sweet.

PLUM AND JUNIPER BERRY TART

Plums peek into northeastern farmers markets towards the end of July. They range from golden orbs to deep purple rounds and either works in this pie. The ground up juniper berry gives it a spice that can be intense!

PREP: 9 MINUTES / ACTIVE: 4 MINUTES / BAKING: 50 MINUTES / TOTAL: 1 HOUR 3 MINUTES / MAKES ONE 9"(23-CM) TART

2 tsp / 7 g dried juniper berries

½ cup / 100 g sugar

1 tsp lemon zest

3 tbsp / 24 g tapioca starch flour

2 lbs (about 7) / 900 g plums, sliced

2 tbsp / 29 ml lemon juice

¼ tsp ground ginger

¼ tsp cinnamon

Preheat the oven to 350°F (175°C).

Prepare Oma's traditional pie dough and your tin (page 25).

In a food processor, blend the juniper berries, sugar and zest together for about 20 seconds, until all the ingredients are chopped and the sugar is fine. Sift the sugar through a fine mesh sieve—to catch the chunks of juniper berry—into a mixing bowl. Stir in the tapioca starch flour.

Toss the plums in the juniper sugar and lemon juice. Pour the filling into your prepared pie shell, top with lattice or design of your choice and bake for 50 minutes, or until golden brown. Allow the pie to cool for at least 2 hours before slicing in.

OPEN-FACED ROASTED CHERRY TART WITH TAHINI-COCOA WHIP AND FRESH CURRANTS

Tahini is a dessert's secret weapon. The sesame paste is featured predominately in hummus, but the nut butter–like consistency is a welcomed ingredient in sweets. It adds a little bit of a toasted essence to the sweetness of the cherries, which deepens the bite. My best friend in Tel Aviv uses tahini in most of her cooking and baking. Time spent with her always exercises the use of the paste and I'm hoping she's impressed by this iteration.

PREP: 10 MINUTES / ACTIVE: 6 MINUTES / BAKING: 45 MINUTES / TOTAL: 1 HOUR 1 MINUTE / MAKES ONE 10"(25-CM) TART

10 oz (about 2 cups) / 288 g, sweet cherries, pitted

1 tbsp / 12 g light brown sugar

1 cup / 236 ml heavy whipping cream

3 tbsp / 23 g confectioners' sugar

3 tsp / 7 g cocoa powder

¼ cup / 78 ml tahini

2 cups / 300 g fresh currants

Preheat the oven to 400°F (205°C).

Prepare Oma's traditional pie dough and pre-bake your pie shell (page 25).

Line a rimmed baking sheet with parchment paper. Toss the cherries with the brown sugar and roast for 30 to 35 minutes, until the cherries have released their juices and begin to naturally caramelize. Let them cool slightly, about 15 minutes.

Whip the cream in a stand mixer at medium speed until frothy, about 1 minute. Slowly add in the confectioners' sugar and cocoa powder with the whisk running on a medium speed, and whip until stiff peaks form, about 3 minutes more. Keep a close eye on the peaks and do not over whip. Fold in the tahini lightly and in increments with a rubber spatula.

Pour the whip into your pre-baked pie shell and let set in the fridge. Top with roasted cherries and fresh currants.

PEACH AND CURRANT REDUCTION PIE

Currants are the kind of tart that makes your face scrunch up. But don't stick your nose up to this pie. Combined with the naturally sweet peach, the currants are a welcomed contrast. Boiled down in fresh orange juice, this pie filling is more like fresh peaches coated in jam. Bite into it and let your taste buds light up like a pinball machine as every chew elicits another flavor. Alternatively, this pie can be made with gooseberries.

PREP: 14 MINUTES / ACTIVE: 8 MINUTES / BAKING: 50 MINUTES / TOTAL: 1 HOUR 12 MINUTES / MAKES ONE 9"(23-CM) PIE

½ cup / 100 g sugar

⅓ cup / 78 ml freshly squeezed orange juice

1 pint / 364 g red currants, stemmed, or 1 cup / 150 g gooseberries

2 lbs (about 5 large) / 900 g peaches, sliced ¼" (6-mm) thick

¼ cup / 33 g tapioca starch flour

Preheat the oven to 350°F (175°C).

Prepare Oma's traditional pie dough and your tin (page 25).

In a small saucepan over medium-high heat, combine the sugar with the orange juice and stir occasionally until dissolved, about 1 minute. Make sure to not bring the liquid to a boil! Add the currants or gooseberries and let them break, about 5 minutes. Reduce the heat to medium-low and continue to cook until the berries begin to thicken, stirring occasionally to avoid burning or sticking to the bottom of the pan, about 9 to 10 minutes. Remove from the heat. Push the mixture through a fine mesh sieve into a large bowl to remove the currant skins and let cool.

Toss the peaches in the currant sauce and mix in the tapioca starch flour. Pour the filling into your prepared pie pan. Top as desired.

Bake for 50 minutes, or until golden brown. Allow the pie to cool on a rack for at least 2 hours before slicing in.

BUTTERMILK PIE WITH RASPBERRY SWIRL

This edible riff on tie-dye is simple and an amusing adornment at summer picnics. Make it a little more "far out" by mixing in multiple purees—blueberry and apricot, for starters. Buttermilk is a canvas here and fruit is the paint. Don't follow the design directions too carefully. Take creative license when playing with purees. You are Pie-casso after all. Whether it looks like a masterpiece or what you thought was a masterpiece in kindergarten, it will still taste like a creamy, soft delight.

PREP: 4 MINUTES 30 SECONDS / ACTIVE: 6 MINUTES / BAKING: 1 HOUR /
TOTAL: 1 HOUR 10 MINUTES / MAKES ONE 10"(25-CM) PIE

½ cup / 100 g sugar

3 eggs

2 tbsp / 16 g tapioca starch flour

¼ tsp cinnamon

2 tsp / 10 ml vanilla extract

1 cup / 236 ml buttermilk

½ cup (1 stick) / 115 g unsalted butter, melted and cooled

2 tbsp / 29 ml raspberry puree

Preheat the oven to 350°F (175°C).

Prepare Oma's traditional pie dough and your tin (page 25).

Whisk the sugar, eggs, tapioca starch flour and cinnamon together. Stir the vanilla into the buttermilk in a measuring cup. Whisk the buttermilk mixture into the sugar. Add the melted and cooled butter, stirring until combined.

Pour into your prepared pie shell and polka dot the buttermilk filling with raspberry puree. With a toothpick, swirl the puree until you get a swirled, tie-dye–like pattern that you're content with.

Bake for 60 minutes. The center should remain a bit wobbly as the buttermilk will continue to set as it cools. Allow the pie to cool on a rack for at least 2 hours before slicing in!

4

FALL

When the leaves turn red, it's the baker's cue to go full speed ahead. Squash swarm market shelves with vibrant meat begging to be roasted in glugs of maple syrup and pleading to glisten under sparkling sugar. This is pie's spotlight season. The crisp air pairs well with a warm slice of appeltaart. Each bite becomes a celebration of the season, like jumping into a heap of just-raked leaves. But most importantly, during fall you'll see your friends and family around the perimeter of the pie, huddled for the traditional gatherings the autumn invites. Autumn's recipes are to be passed around, shared and are best served in a loud room of sweater-clad company. My go-to recipes for a gathering or a chilly day inside are the classic Traditional Dutch Appeltaart (page 81), Dairy-Free Date-Sweetened Squash Pie (page 84) and the Sesame Pumpkin Pie with Chocolate-Tahini Swirl (page 98). I recommend preparing all appeltaarts in a deep-dish springform pan, but you can also use a traditional 10-inch (25-cm) pie plate to fit as many apple slices in as possible!

TRADITIONAL DUTCH APPELTAART

Oma promised that if you peel an apple skin perfectly in one swirl, toss it over your head and let it land on the floor, the shape it takes will be the first initial of your soul mate. I grew up swinging Granny Smith peels over my head as if practicing for the rodeo. (My soul mate's initial has typically been revealed as a vague "N," or maybe "S" if you cock your head.) This fortune-telling technique is one of the many pleasures in composing the traditional taart.

Whether your peel spells out your future romance or not, there will certainly be a lot of love surrounding Oma's traditional, simple Dutch delight. I keep coming back to this recipe time after time for dinner parties, Thanksgiving feasts and just another weekend night. The thinly sliced apples create crepe-cake-like layers that will turn an apple pie hater into an enthusiast, as chunks don't overwhelm the bite. The tart crunch of apples supported by the sweet crust invigorates the taste buds. Add the cool factor of vanilla ice cream on top and suddenly a bite of pie becomes more like a love potion.

PREP: 15 MINUTES / ACTIVE: 5 MINUTES / BAKING: 50 MINUTES / TOTAL: 1 HOUR 10 MINUTES / MAKES ONE 9"(23-CM) PIE

2¼ lbs (about 4 to 5 apples) / 1 kg tart apples (Mutsu or Granny Smith), peeled and sliced ¼"(6-mm) thin

1 tbsp / 14 ml lemon juice

3 tbsp / 37 g granulated sugar

2 tbsp / 16 g ground cinnamon

1 tsp salt

Vanilla ice cream, for serving, optional

Whipped cream, for serving, optional

Preheat the oven to 350°F (175°C).

Prepare Oma's traditional pie dough and your tin (page 25).

Using your hands, toss the apples in a mixing bowl with the lemon juice, sugar, cinnamon and salt. Try one! If you want them to be a little sweeter, add a teaspoon of sugar at a time and toss to distribute the added sweetness.

Spread the apple filling evenly in the prepared pie pan and top with a lattice or inspired design of your choice. If you'd like to try a rose design, see page 94.

Bake for 45 to 50 minutes, until the top is golden brown. Allow the pie to cool in the pan for 30 to 35 minutes. The liquid released from the apples will continue to cook and thicken as you patiently wait with your fork nearby.

Enjoy with a scoop of vanilla ice cream or homemade whipped cream.

TIPS: You can use a mandolin when slicing the apples to get a consistently thin slice. But a sharp paring knife and eye for detail will work well here too.

You can use a 9-inch (23-cm) pie pan, but traditionally a springform pan is used in Holland to create more of a deep-dish style apple pie.

ZUCCA PIE (TRADITIONAL PUMPKIN PIE)

In Tuscany, I spent autumn days clipping pumpkins and squash from their stalks. We stocked up on over 300 kilograms for winter to make risotto, sauces, mashes and—if I was going to have my way—pie. Multiple variations of pumpkin grew in the field where chickens roamed. These chickens nurtured the soil that the squash organically bloomed from. They did the hard part. The soil gave the squash its flavor. Putting everything else together is a piece of...well, pie.

The fresh pumpkin puree can be enjoyed by the spoonful alone, full of fresh fall flavor. But when baked, its silky, spicy custard will make you happy that you waited for the baked forkful.

PREP: 4 MINUTES / ACTIVE: 3 MINUTES / BAKING: 75 MINUTES / TOTAL: 2 HOURS 7 MINUTES / MAKES TWO 9"(23-CM) PIES

1 sugar pumpkin, or 13.3 oz (about 1½ cups) / 376 ml pumpkin puree

½ cup / 118 ml dark grade A maple syrup

1 tsp vanilla extract

1 tsp ground cinnamon

¼ tsp ground nutmeg

¼ tsp ground cloves

¼ tsp ground ginger

¼ tsp ground cardamom

¼ cup / 50 g dark brown sugar

¼ cup / 50 g sugar

2 large eggs

¾ cups / 177 ml heavy cream

Vanilla ice cream, for serving, optional

Whipped cream, for serving, optional

Preheat the oven to 350°F (175°C).

Prepare Oma's traditional pie dough and your tin (page 25).

Cut a sugar pumpkin, preferably from your farmers market or local pumpkin patch, in half and remove the seeds as well as the fibers. Place it cut side down on a baking sheet and bake until it's fork tender, about 45 to 50 minutes. Let the baked pumpkin cool, peel off the skin and then transfer the meat to a food processer or powerful blender. Blend until pureed.

In a large bowl, combine the pumpkin puree, maple syrup and vanilla. In a separate bowl, whisk the spices into the sugars until uniform. Stir the spice mixture into the pumpkin mixture, followed by the eggs and cream, whisking together until you have one large bowl of rusty orange liquid.

Pour the filling into the prepared pie shell, just under the brim. The filling will rise when baking, and this will help you avoid a mess when squatting down to evenly place it into the oven.

Bake for 75 minutes. Check to see if the crust is browning after 15 minutes. If it looks nearly perfect or begins to burn before the custard is set, cover with a pie shield or tin foil.

Allow the pie to cool for at least 2 hours on a rack before slicing in, and serve with a scoop of vanilla ice cream or freshly whipped cream.

> TIP: Combine the spices together ahead of time, even when you aren't in the mood for pie, to have on hand for lattes and pancakes. Use an old spice container for your new homemade pumpkin spice.

MAPLE PUMPKIN PIE

There are many ways to make a pumpkin vary in flavor and levels of sweetness. Maple sugar and maple syrup are my go-to tools in my sweetener arsenal. Popular around the northeast of the United States, the sugar is made from a maple tree's sap. It's boiled down into maple syrup that can be used in place of granulated sugar and makes everything taste like Vermont, a place where people value evergreens, smiling, ice cream and homegrown foods. This pie tastes like foliage looks, robust and delectable.

PREP: 4 MINUTES / ACTIVE: 3 MINUTES / BAKING: 75 MINUTES / TOTAL: 2 HOURS 7 MINUTES / MAKES TWO 9"(23-CM) PIES

1 sugar pumpkin or 1½ cups / 372 ml pumpkin puree

¼ cup / 50 g maple sugar

¼ cup / 50 g dark brown sugar

1 tsp ground cinnamon

¼ tsp ground nutmeg

¼ tsp ground cloves

¼ tsp ground ginger

¼ tsp ground cardamom

½ cup + 2 tbsp / 147 ml dark maple syrup

2 tsp / 10 ml vanilla extract

¾ cup / 177 ml heavy cream

2 large eggs

Vanilla ice cream, for serving, optional

Whipped cream, for serving, optional

Preheat the oven to 350°F (175°C).

Prepare Oma's traditional pie dough and your tin (page 25).

Cut a sugar pumpkin (preferably from your farmers market or local pumpkin patch) in half and remove the seeds as well as the fibers. Place the cut side down on a baking sheet and bake until it's fork tender, about 45 to 50 minutes. Let the baked pumpkin cool, peel off the skin and then transfer the meat to a food processer or powerful blender. Blend until pureed.

Combine the pumpkin puree with the maple sugar, brown sugar, spices, maple syrup and vanilla. Whisk together until combined.

Slowly stir in the heavy cream a little bit at a time. Whisk in the eggs until everything is thoroughly combined.

Pour the custard into your prepared pie shell. Bake for 75 minutes. Check to see if the crust is browning after 15 minutes. If it looks nearly perfect or begins to burn before the custard is set, cover with a pie shield or tin foil.

Allow the pie to cool on a rack for at least 2 hours and serve with a scoop of vanilla ice cream or freshly whipped cream!

TIP: Combine the spices together ahead of time, even when you aren't in the mood for pie, to have on hand for lattes and pancakes. Use an old spice container for your new homemade pumpkin spice.

DAIRY-FREE DATE-SWEETENED SQUASH PIE

This pie is absent of granulated sugar. It's sweetened by a date puree instead. Once I grew up and gave dates a try while avoiding sugar, I realized they weren't just oddly shaped dried things; they're really good.

For those who have stomachs averse to heavy cream—an ingredient heavily featured in pumpkin custards—this butternut squash pie tastes just like any other except with a little something extra thanks to the coconut cream. The cream lends its silkiness to the overall texture of the pie, which becomes too easy for forks to slide through.

PREP: 59 MINUTES / ACTIVE: 5 MINUTES / BAKING: 55–60 MINUTES / TOTAL: 2 HOUR 4 MINUTES / MAKES ONE 9"(23-CM) PIE

1 butternut squash, yields about 2 lbs (1½ cups) / 372 ml butternut squash puree

¾ cup (about 15–16 dates)/ 140 g pitted dates

½ cup / 118 ml water, divided

1 tsp ground cinnamon

¼ tsp ground ginger

¼ tsp ground cardamom

¼ tsp ground nutmeg

⅛ tsp ground cloves

½ cup / 118 ml dark maple syrup

¾ cup / 117 ml coconut cream

2 tsp / 10 ml vanilla extract

3 large eggs

Dairy-free ice cream, for serving, optional

Preheat the oven to 350°F (175°C).

Prepare Oma's traditional pie dough and your tin (page 25).

Cut a butternut squash (preferably from your farmers market or local pumpkin patch) in half and remove the seeds as well as the fibers. Place the cut side down on a baking sheet and bake until fork tender, about 45 to 50 minutes. Let the baked squash cool, peel off the skin and then transfer the meat to a food processer or powerful blender. Blend until pureed.

To make the date puree, cover the dates with ½ cup (118 ml) of water and microwave for 60 seconds. It's important not to cook the dates too long or you'll end up with nuclear dates that'll be too mushy to puree. You can also cover the dates with water in a mason jar and let them soak overnight. Transfer the dates and ¼ cup (59 ml) of the water to a food processor or blender and puree until you have a smooth paste, about 3 minutes.

Fold the date puree into the squash, followed by the spices and maple syrup. Whisk in the coconut cream until smooth, followed by the vanilla and eggs, one egg at a time.

Pour into a prepared pie shell and bake for 55 to 60 minutes, or until the crust is golden brown and the center of the pie is just about set.

Allow the pie to cool on a rack for about 2 hours before slicing in. Serve with dairy-free ice ceam.

CHEESY PEAR AND FIG PIE

This pie teeters on the edge of sweet and savory. The cooked pears soften under the ricotta, making each bite reminiscent of your favorite breakfast toast topping.

In Italy, we picked figs on our walk down to the gardens or on our way back from a morning jog before work. They grow abundantly on the side of Tuscan roads where you'll likely drive past the scenery of women on ladders picking what they can reach. We climbed trees and dropped the good, plump, oozing ones down. When you bite into a fig, it looks kind of like what you'd imagine the inside of an alien's mouth would, but I promise you it tastes nothing like that image. It's like honey and maple syrup if both were a fruit. Back in Brooklyn, I am closely watching the figs that grow in a neighbor's gated front yard because when they're ripe, it won't be sugar I'll be asking for.

PREP: 13 MINUTES / ACTIVE: 7 MINUTES / BAKING: 45–50 MINUTES / TOTAL: 1 HOUR 5 MINUTES / MAKES ONE 9"(23-CM) PIE

¼ cup / 137 g ricotta

1½ tbsp / 22 ml lemon juice

¼ cup + 1 tbsp / 75 g dark brown sugar

½ tsp cinnamon

⅛ tsp nutmeg

⅛ tsp ground cloves

1 lb 8 oz (about 4) / 660 g D'Anjou pears, thinly sliced

5 oz (about 4) / 140 g figs, quartered

Drizzle of honey

Preheat the oven to 350°F (175°C).

Prepare Oma's traditional pie dough and your tin (page 25).

Using a rubber spatula, combine the ricotta with lemon juice, brown sugar, cinnamon, nutmeg and cloves in a small bowl. In a larger bowl, pour the sweet ricotta over the sliced pears and toss to combine until the slices are completely doused in the cheese.

Arrange the pears into a rose-like pattern in your prepared pie shell (page 94), top with figs and drizzle honey in a spiral on top of the fruit. Leave uncovered or top with a lattice or inspired design.

Bake for 45 to 50 minutes. Allow the pie to cool on a rack for at least 2 hours before slicing in!

HONEYNUT SQUASH PIE

On the side of the road in the Catskills region of New York, I pulled into a pumpkin patch across from a horse barn. I went with the intention of purchasing a sugar pumpkin but left with a sweater full of honeynut squash. The squash hybrid was developed by Blue Hill's Dan Barber and plant breeder Michael Mazourek. It's a miniature butternut squash but size doesn't matter here. Though small, it packs flavor under its skin.

You can find these guys hanging around New York farmers markets, and seeds are available for purchase so you can grow your own and make this a very homegrown pie tailored to your region.

PREP: 2 MINUTES / ACTIVE: 2 MINUTES / BAKING: 65 MINUTES / TOTAL: 1 HOUR 54 MINUTES / MAKES ONE 9"(23-CM) PIE

2 honeynut squash, yields 1½ cups / 350 ml honeynut squash puree

¼ cup / 50 g dark brown sugar

½ tsp cinnamon

¼ tsp ginger

¼ tsp cardamom

1 tsp vanilla extract

2 tbsp / 29 ml honey

¾ cups / 177 ml heavy cream

2 extra-large eggs

Preheat the oven to 350°F (175°C).

Prepare Oma's traditional pie dough and your tin (page 25).

Cut the honeynut squash (preferably from your farmers market or local pumpkin patch or backyard garden) in half lengthwise and remove the seeds as well as the fibers. Place the cut side down on a baking sheet and bake until fork tender, about 45 to 50 minutes. Let the baked squash cool, peel off the skin and then transfer the meat to a food processer or powerful blender. Blend until pureed.

Combine the puree with the brown sugar, spices, vanilla and honey. Whisk in the heavy cream gradually and, once thoroughly combined, whisk in the eggs one at a time.

Pour the custard into your prepared pie shell. Bake for 65 to 70 minutes, until the custard is just wobbly in the center. Allow the pie to cool on a rack for at least 2 hours before slicing in.

TIP: If you can't find a honeynut, you can use butternut squash! Sweeten a little more with 2 tablespoons (29 ml) of honey.

GINGERED PEAR PIE

Pear pie is a classic cousin to apple. Less of a crunch and more of a soft bite, the pear pie becomes more of a palatable mash mid-chew.

When I was growing up, my great-grandmother and great-Oma would visit and head straight for our backyard where a towering pear tree still reigns today. They'd pick the fruit and sit under the tree in hunter-green kitchen chairs with a bowl beneath their knees, peeling the pears before bringing the fruit in for a cobbler.

PREP: 25 MINUTES / ACTIVE: 5 MINUTES / BAKING: 50 MINUTES / TOTAL: 1 HOUR, 20 MINUTES / MAKES ONE 9"(23-CM) PIE

2 lbs (about 5–6) / 907 g D'Anjou pears, peeled, cored and thinly sliced

2 tbsp / 29 ml lemon juice

1 tsp cinnamon

2 tbsp / 25 g light brown sugar

2 tsp / 10 g freshly grated ginger

¼ tsp nutmeg

3 tbsp / 24 g arrowroot starch flour

Ice cream, for serving, optional

Preheat the oven to 350°F (175°C).

Prepare Oma's traditional pie dough and your tin (page 25).

Toss the pears with lemon juice, cinnamon, brown sugar, ginger, nutmeg and arrowroot.

Pour the mixture into a prepared pie shell and top with a lattice or design of your choice.

Bake the pie for 50 minutes, or until the crust is golden brown.

Allow the pie to cool on a rack for at least 1 hour before enjoying with a scoop of ice cream.

BROWN SUGAR PEAR AND ROSEMARY GOAT CHEESE TART

Pears and cheese don't get enough credit compared to salt and pepper or peanut butter and jelly. We eat the combination together on top of pizzas and on crackers. Think of this pie as one big appetizer cracker, except with more maple syrup and brown sugar. Plus, it's a little more involved than just tossing two ingredients on top of a round cracker.

The creamy texture of the whipped cheeses inside the shell absorb the dripping sugars from the pears like a welcome leak only possible in your dreams. It's a pie that has a place on both the appetizer and dessert table at your next shindig.

PREP: 6 MINUTES / ACTIVE: 6 MINUTES / BAKING: 25 MINUTES / TOTAL: 37 MINUTES / MAKES ONE TART

1 lb (about 3) / 450 g D'Anjou pears, halved

2 tbsp / 27 g light brown sugar, packed

1 tbsp / 14 ml maple syrup

1 cup / 150 g plain goat cheese, softened

¼ cup / 55 g cream cheese, softened

¼ tsp salt

2 tbsp / 5 g rosemary leaves, finely chopped

Preheat the oven to 350°F (175°C).

Prepare Oma's traditional pie dough and pre-bake the crust (page 25).

Smear the pears with brown sugar and maple syrup. Bake with the cut side down in a 9 x 13-inch (23 cm x 33-cm) baking dish for 20 to 25 minutes, until slightly caramelized. Remove the pears from the oven and let them cool.

Whip the goat cheese, cream cheese, salt and rosemary in a stand mixer until creamy, about 2 minutes. If you don't have a stand mixer, you can beat the ingredients together with a wooden spoon in a mixing bowl.

Spread the whipped cheese mixture in the pre-baked pie shell. Slice the pears and arrange them on top. Let set in the fridge for at least 1 hour.

LONG ISLAND "ICED TEA" CHEESE PUMPKIN PIE

At first bite, you might not think there's anything different about this pumpkin pie. But it will hit you, as Long Island Iced Teas typically do. A rush of liquor hits that, while not overwhelming or too intense, most certainly makes its presence known. It's a new, autumn rift on a bourbon pie.

The Long Island Cheese pumpkin is used here and the heirloom variety is known for being one of the oldest varieties found in America. This pumpkin is greatly different from the carving kind, and while it's not perfectly orange and round as we have come to imagine a pumpkin, it is stumpy with extra grooves. It looks like it could be painted by Dutch painter Pieter Claesz. But besides rustic beauty, the squash was pivotal in maintaining the health of the land in which food was grown to feed a community. You can buy your own Long Island Cheese pumpkin heirloom seeds through the Hudson Valley Seed Company.

Make this pumpkin pie to share with your community (aged 21+).

PREP: 4 MINUTES / ACTIVE: 3 MINUTES / BAKING: 70–75 MINUTES / TOTAL: 2 HOURS 7 MINUTES / MAKES TWO 9"(23-CM) PIES

1 medium Long Island Cheese pumpkin, (about 1½ cups / 376 ml pumpkin puree)

¾ cup / 170 g light brown sugar

½ tsp cinnamon

½ tsp ginger

½ tsp nutmeg

⅔ cup / 157 g heavy cream

2 tbsp / 29 ml maple syrup

1 tbsp / 14 ml gin

1 tbsp / 14 ml rum

2 large eggs

Preheat the oven to 350°F (175°C).

Prepare Oma's traditional pie dough and your tin (page 25).

Cut a pumpkin (preferably from your farmers market or local pumpkin patch) in half and remove the seeds as well as fibers. Place the cut side down on a baking sheet and bake until fork tender, about 45 to 50 minutes. Let the baked pumpkin cool, peel off the skin and then transfer the meat to a food processer or powerful blender. Blend until pureed.

Whisk the light brown sugar and spices together. Whisk in the heavy cream and maple syrup and then gradually stir into the pumpkin puree followed by the gin and rum. Whisk in the eggs, one at a time, until thoroughly incorporated.

Pour the custard into your prepared pie shell. Bake for 70 to 75 minutes until the crust is golden brown and the custard is just about set in the center. Allow the pie to cool on a rack for at least 2 hours before slicing in.

HERBED APPLE PIE

Herbs are a kitchen dweller's best friend. They take something good and make it better. Even apple pie. Smearing slices with an herb-infused butter makes each bite something to savor, as the flavors run deep and soak each tart slice with their essence.

PREP: 20 MINUTES / ACTIVE: 5 MINUTES / BAKING: 50 MINUTES / TOTAL: 1 HOUR 15 MINUTES / MAKES ONE 9"(23-CM) PIE

1 tbsp / 15 g rosemary, finely chopped

2 tsp / 10 g thyme, finely chopped

⅛ tsp salt

2 tbsp / 29 ml lemon juice

½ cup (1 stick) / 115 g unsalted butter, softened

2 lbs (about 5) / 907 g tart apples such as Mutsu or Granny Smith, peeled and thinly sliced

¼ cup / 50 g light brown sugar

Vanilla ice cream, for serving, optional

Preheat the oven to 350°F (175°C).

Prepare Oma's traditional pie dough and your tin (page 25).

Make a compound butter by folding the finely chopped herbs, salt and lemon juice into the softened butter with a small rubber spatula or the back of a cereal spoon in a small mixing bowl. Fold until the herbs are distributed throughout the butter.

Toss the apples with the herbed compound butter and brown sugar, making sure to smear all the apple slices.

Pour the buttered apples into your prepared pie shell and add a lattice crust, if desired. Bake for 50 minutes, until the crust is golden brown.

Allow the pie to cool on a rack for at least 1 hour before slicing in and enjoying with a scoop of vanilla ice cream.

TIP: You can use a mandolin when slicing the apples to get a consistently thin slice. But a sharp paring knife and eye for detail will work well here too.

To achieve a rose-shaped design for your apple pie, take the thinly sliced apples and begin by building a border inside the pie's walls. Use the thicker ones here, as they're not as flexible as the ones you'll need for the middle! Continue to layer, staggering the apple slices as you move in so that the top rounds of the slices are peeking through the ones behind it. When you get towards the center, bend your slices into "C" shapes to fit as many apples as you can in. The more slices, the more robust the rose design, and the more likely your friends will be impressed. Roll the thinnest slice, usually from the end of a quartered apple chunk, into a cigar and stick it in the middle. Voilà, you have a freshly bloomed floral that carries the scent of cinnamon.

APPLE PIE WITH OATMEAL CRUMBLE

Peeling apples takes up most of the prep time here. Grab a friend to feed slices to as they keep you company. Thinly sliced apples convert apple pie naysayers into fans. This version of the appeltaart has more of an American topping and familiarity, while also continuing to cling to Dutch spices, more of which are seen in this pie than in the traditional version.

PREP: 20 MINUTES / ACTIVE: 5 MINUTES / BAKING: 50 MINUTES / TOTAL: 1 HOUR 15 MINUTES / MAKES ONE 9–10" (23–25-CM) PIE

2 lbs (about 4–5) / 907 g tart apples, such as Mutsu or Granny Smith, peeled and thinly sliced

2 tbsp / 29 ml lemon juice

1 tsp cinnamon

¼ tsp cardamom

¼ tsp nutmeg

⅛ tsp ground cloves

¼ cup / 50 g dark brown sugar

2 tbsp / 25 g granulated sugar

Vanilla ice cream, for serving, optional

OATMEAL CRUMBLE

1 cup / 80 g old-fashioned oats

½ cup / 120 g unbleached all-purpose flour

3 tbsp / 37 g light brown sugar

1 tsp cinnamon

½ cup (1 stick) / 115 g unsalted butter, cut into cubes

¼ tsp salt

Preheat the oven to 350°F (175°C).

Prepare Oma's traditional pie dough and your tin (page 25).

Combine the apple slices with the lemon juice, spices and sugars.

Pour the filling into your prepared pie shell.

For the oatmeal crumble topping, mix the oats, flour, sugar and cinnamon together. Toss in the butter and work into the flour with your hands until the butter is broken down and varies in size from peas to dimes. Spread evenly over the apples.

Bake for 45 to 50 minutes, until the crust is golden brown.

Allow the pie to cool on a rack for up to 1 hour and enjoy topped with a scoop of vanilla ice cream.

TIP: You can use a mandolin when slicing the apples to get a consistently thin slice. A sharp paring knife and eye for detail will work well here too.

SESAME PUMPKIN PIE WITH CHOCOLATE-TAHINI SWIRL

For those who can't enjoy Nutella (which includes myself), there is a cheat code in the form of tahini and chocolate. The roasted sesame paste mixed into the chocolate gives that thick and goopy goodness you can spread on everything or eat straight from the bowl.

The sesame flavors swirled into the squash add a toasted nuttiness that satisfies in so many ways for more than just the allergen-abled people.

PREP: 4 MINUTES / ACTIVE: 3 MINUTES / BAKING: 70–75 MINUTES / TOTAL: 2 HOURS 7 MINUTES / MAKES ONE 10"(25-CM) PIE

1 small sugar pumpkin, or 1½ cups / 376 ml pumpkin puree

½ cup / 101 g light brown sugar

1 tsp ground cinnamon

¼ tsp ground nutmeg

¼ tsp ground cloves

¼ tsp ground ginger

¼ tsp ground cardamom

2 tbsp / 29 ml honey

2 tbsp / 29 ml maple syrup

1 tsp vanilla extract

¾ cup / 177 ml heavy cream

2 large eggs

1 tbsp / 14 ml tahini

2 tsp / 7 g sesame seeds

Whipped cream, for serving, optional

CHOCOLATE-TAHINI SAUCE
2 oz / 56 g dark chocolate (68%)

1 tbsp / 14 ml tahini

⅛ tsp salt

Preheat the oven to 350°F (175°C).

Prepare Oma's traditional pie dough and your tin (page 25).

Cut a sugar pumpkin (preferably from your farmers market or local pumpkin patch) in half and remove the seeds as well as the fibers. Place the cut side down on a baking sheet and bake until fork tender, about 45 to 50 minutes. Let the baked pumpkin cool, peel off the skin and then transfer the meat to a food processer or powerful blender. Blend until pureed.

Combine the pumpkin puree with the brown sugar, spices, honey, maple syrup, vanilla, heavy cream, eggs, tahini and sesame seeds.

To make the sauce, melt the chocolate in a double boiler or a heatproof bowl set over a pot of boiling water. Fold in the tahini and salt with a rubber spatula until everything is combined in nutty-chocolatey glory.

Pour the pumpkin filling into a prepared pie shell. Dollop the chocolate over it and swirl it into the custard with a toothpick.

Bake for 70 to 75 minutes. Check to see if the crust is browning after 15 minutes. If it looks nearly perfect or begins to burn before the custard is set, cover with a pie shield or tin foil.

Allow the pie to cool for up to 2 hours before slicing in and enjoying with a dollop of freshly whipped cream!

PLAIN OL' PEAR PIE

Sometimes the best way to go is the way of simplicity. Let flavors do their job and stand out without much support of anything else. Not a lot com-pears to biting into one of these fresh fruits. They're sweet and make for an exciting pie texture. If you're one for enjoying things as they are, this is the pie for you.

PREP: 25 MINUTES / ACTIVE: 4 MINUTES / BAKING: 50 MINUTES / TOTAL: 1 HOUR 19 MINUTES / MAKES ONE 10" (25-CM) PIE

2 lbs (about 5–6) / 907 g D'Anjou pears, peeled and thinly sliced

2 tbsp / 29 ml lemon juice

¼ cup / 50 g granulated sugar

2 tbsp / 25 g light brown sugar

¼ tsp ground cloves

¼ tsp cinnamon

Vanilla ice cream, for serving, optional

Preheat the oven to 350°F (175°C).

Prepare Oma's traditional pie dough and your tin (page 25).

Toss the pears with lemon juice, sugar, brown sugar, cloves and cinnamon. Pour the filling into the prepared pie shell and top with a lattice or design of your choice.

Bake for 50 minutes, or until crust is golden brown.

Allow the pie to cool on a rack for up to 1 hour before enjoying with a scoop of vanilla ice cream.

PUMPKIN FIG PIE

The smooth texture of the pumpkin custard is a perfect pillow for the figs floating on top. While baking, they sink in, seeping their sweetness towards the bottom of the crust to fill the pie further with flavor. The sprinkled brown sugar on top helps caramelize the figs. This is the perfect pie to keep you warm and full on the first chilled day of fall.

PREP: 4 MINUTES / ACTIVE: 3 MINUTES / BAKING: 75 MINUTES / TOTAL: 2 HOURS 7 MINUTES / MAKES ONE 10" (25-CM) PIE

1 sugar pumpkin, or 1½ cups / 376 ml pumpkin puree

½ cup / 101 g light brown sugar, plus more for sprinkling

½ tsp ground cinnamon

¼ tsp ground ginger

¼ tsp ground cardamom

¼ tsp ground cloves

¼ tsp ground nutmeg

½ cup / 118 ml dark maple syrup

¾ cup / 177 ml heavy cream

2 large eggs

4.2 oz (about 4) / 118 g figs, sliced into coins

Vanilla ice cream, for serving, optional

Whipped cream, for serving, optional

Preheat the oven to 350°F (175°C).

Prepare Oma's traditional pie dough and your tin (page 25).

Cut a sugar pumpkin (preferably from your farmers market or local pumpkin patch) in half and remove the seeds as well as the fibers. Place the cut side down on a baking sheet and bake until fork tender, about 45 to 50 minutes. Let the baked pumpkin cool, peel off the skin and then transfer the meat to a food processer or powerful blender. Blend until pureed.

Whisk in the brown sugar, spices and maple syrup. Slowly incorporate the heavy cream until thoroughly combined, followed by the eggs, whisked in one at a time. Pour the custard into your prepared pie shell.

Arrange the sliced figs on top of the custard. Sprinkle brown sugar over the figs and custard.

Bake for 75 minutes. Check to see if the crust is browning after 15 minutes. If it looks nearly perfect or begins to burn before the custard is set, cover with a pie shield or tin foil. This will prevent the crust from burning while still cooking the custard.

Allow the pie to cool on a rack for at least 2 hours before serving with a scoop of vanilla ice cream or freshly whipped cream!

TIP: Combine the spices together ahead of time, even when you aren't in the mood for pie, to have on hand for lattes and pancakes. Use an old spice container for your new homemade pumpkin spice.

LAVENDER ZUCCA PIE

This taart is dedicated to a baker named Pietrina, who made a pumpkin lavender cake that I fawned over and enjoyed so much that my friends kindly gave their slices up so I could continue to chew bliss. While I'm not sure how she made it, I began my mission to make something of the same flavor combination half as a good as Pietrina made.

PREP: 4 MINUTES / ACTIVE: 3 MINUTES / BAKE: 75 MINUTES / TOTAL: 1 HOUR 22 MINUTES / MAKES ONE 10" (25-CM) PIE

1 sugar pumpkin, or 13.3 oz (about 1½ cups) / 376 ml pumpkin puree

¾ cup / 177 ml heavy cream

1 tbsp + 2 tsp / 5 g dried lavender buds, divided

½ cup / 107 g granulated sugar

1 tsp ground cinnamon

¼ tsp ground nutmeg

¼ tsp ground cloves

¼ tsp ground ginger

¼ tsp ground cardamom

½ cup / 118 ml dark grade A maple syrup

1 tsp vanilla extract

2 large eggs

Vanilla ice cream, for serving, optional

Whipped cream, for serving, optional

> **TIP:** Combine the spices together ahead of time, even when you aren't in the mood for pie, to have on hand for lattes and pancakes. Use an old spice container for your new homemade pumpkin spice.

Preheat the oven to 350°F (175°C).

Prepare Oma's traditional pie dough and your tin (page 25).

Cut a sugar pumpkin (preferably from your farmers market or local pumpkin patch) in half and remove the seeds as well as the fibers. Place the cut side down on a baking sheet and bake until fork tender, about 45 to 50 minutes.

Meanwhile, warm the heavy cream over medium heat in a medium saucepan with 1 tablespoon (3 g) of lavender buds, but do not bring to a boil. Stir occasionally to prevent burning and once steam starts to rise from the heavy cream, remove the saucepan from the heat and allow the lavender to steep for 30 minutes. Strain the heavy cream through a fine mesh sieve to remove the lavender buds. Let cool.

Let the baked pumpkin cool and then transfer the meat to a food processor or powerful blender. Blend until pureed. It should essentially look like baby food.

In a clean food processor, pulse the sugar and remaining lavender until the lavender is broken down and incorporated into the sugar.

In a small bowl, whisk the spices into the sugar until uniform. In a large bowl, combine the pumpkin puree, maple syrup and vanilla. Stir in the spiced sugar mixture, followed by the cream and then eggs one at a time, whisking together until you have one large bowl of rusty orange liquid.

Bake for 75 minutes. Check to see if the crust is browning after 30 minutes. If it looks nearly perfect or begins to burn before the custard is set, cover with a pie shield or tin foil. This will prevent the crust from burning as the filling continues to cook.

Allow the pie to cool on a rack for at least 2 hours before serving with a scoop of vanilla ice cream or freshly whipped cream!

VENDEMMIA PIE

After spending three days in the vineyards plucking grapes from the vine, our hands were stained purple and stuck to everything we touched. The farm had a lunch to celebrate the success of *Vendemmia*, the Italian grape harvest, where we raised a glass to all the hard work of the people before us. The people who protected the vines from *cinghiale*, or wild boar, and kept them healthy until this successful conclusion. At the end of our lunch, where a portrait of Bacchus reigned at the head of the table, we were treated to a grape dessert that was rich and jam-like. The grapes weren't seedless so every bite left us spitting but it was worth it.

This pie is along the lines of a *crostata di uva*, an Italian pie-like dessert with a jam filling.

PREP: 28 MINUTES / ACTIVE: 3 MINUTES / BAKING: 50–55 MINUTES / TOTAL: 1 HOUR 35 MINUTES / MAKES ONE 8" (20-CM) PIE

2½ lbs (about 6½ to 7 cups) / 1.1 kg concord grapes

½ cup / 100 g granulated sugar

2 tbsp / 29 ml castagno honey

Juice of ½ a lemon

Preheat the oven to 400°F (205°C).

Prepare Oma's traditional pie dough and your tin (page 25).

Separate the skins from the pulp of the grape by squeezing one end. The pulp should slip right out! Place the skins into a food processor and pulse until they're broken down, about 1 minute. Transfer the chopped skins to a bowl.

Put the grape pulp into a medium saucepan and cook them over medium heat until they're translucent and spitting out their seeds, about 8 to 10 minutes. Remove the pan from the heat and press the pulp through a fine mesh sieve into a mixing bowl with the back of a wooden spoon. This will catch the grape seeds. Mix the grape skins into the pulp and transfer the combination to a clean medium saucepan. Mix in the sugar, honey and lemon juice, and cook over medium heat for about 20 to 25 minutes, until the mixture has begun to thicken. This will give the grapes that deep purple hue and jam-like consistency.

Pour the filling into your prepared pie tin and top with a lattice or inspired design of your choice.

Bake for 15 minutes and then reduce the temperature to 325°F (163°C), and cook until the filling is set, about 35 to 40 minutes.

Allow the pie to cool for up to 2 hours before slicing in.

TIP: If you don't have a fine mesh sieve, you can use a colander to catch the seeds.

5

WINTER

Oma always visits in the winter. New York isn't much of an escape from Toronto's trenches of snow, but freezing temperatures don't matter when your entire family is together. Growing up, Oma would keep us warm with double grilled cheese sandwiches while balancing our nutrition with a bottomless bowl of apple wedges. Oma made winter the warmest season.

Bake these pies for your friends, for your family or for that bartender you have a crush on. Give them out as presents, as offerings and as conversation starters. Or bake one for yourself when you're really hungry and just want to feel okay. However you use these recipes, just bake it like you mean it. When I need a rich dessert to sink into the couch with, I whip up a chocolate pie like the Egg-Free Rosemary Chocolate Silk Pie (page 127), or I like to warm up with a Speculaas Parsnip (page 112) or Brown Butter Maple Carrot (page 115) pie. I hope you too find your perfect pie to cuddle up with this winter.

BEET-RED WHITE CHOCOLATE PIE

Beets. If you're one of the people who despises beets, you might be taken by this pie. The "dirt"-like taste—which we'll just call "earth"—is eliminated through the process of roasting and bonding with sugar. Beets are a root vegetable that are naturally sweet and ever giving to our nutrition. You can use their greens in smoothies and salads. To further their use in the kitchen, this pie was bred out of curiosity and infatuation with the color the produce wears. The pie has a smooth, almost jelly-like, feel to it. I hope your heart beets for it.

PREP: 12 MINUTES / ACTIVE: 6 MINUTES / BAKING: 55–60 MINUTES / TOTAL: 1 HOUR 18 MINUTES / MAKES ONE 10" (25-CM) PIE

4 small-medium beets, washed, yields 1½ cups (about 1 lb) / 360 ml beet puree

1 tbsp / 14 ml honey

½ cup / 101 g granulated sugar

¾ cup / 177 ml heavy cream

3 eggs

2 oz / 56 g white chocolate, coarsely chopped and melted

Preheat the oven to 350°F (175°C).

Prepare Oma's traditional pie dough and your tin (page 25).

Wrap your washed beets in tin foil and arrange them on a baking sheet. Roast the beets for 1 hour, or until they can be easily pierced by a fork.

Peel the skin off the beets and admire your new pink hands. Cube the beets and transfer them to a food processor or powerful blender to puree, about 3 to 5 minutes, until completely smooth.

Transfer the puree to a medium mixing bowl and whisk in the honey and sugar, followed by the heavy cream and eggs, one at a time.

Pour the filling into your prepared pie shell and polka dot the fuchsia-pink filling with white chocolate. Using a toothpick, create white swirls to your liking.

Bake for 55 to 60 minutes and allow the pie to cool on a rack for at least 2 hours before slicing in!

CRANBERRY TEA CURD TART

The maroon hue of this pie is sure to stun dinner party guests this winter. It also gives those bags of cranberries you gratefully pick up from the market or freeze from the fall haul a new lease on life outside their expected dishes. Letting chai spices steep allows the cranberry tart to warm up, making this the perfect slice to curl up with in front of the fireplace.

PREP: 5 MINUTES / ACTIVE: 11 MINUTES / TOTAL: 28 MINUTES / MAKES ONE 8" (20-CM) TART

¾ cup / 150 g granulated sugar, divided

½ cup / 118 ml water

12 oz (about 3 cups) / 300 g fresh cranberries

2 chai spice tea bags

¼ cup / 59 ml fresh orange juice

2 large eggs

4 large egg yolks

Zest from one orange

Prepare Oma's traditional pie dough and pre-bake your crust (page 25).

In a medium saucepan over medium-high heat, stir ½ cup (100 g) of sugar into the water, add the cranberries and bring to a boil. Reduce the heat to medium-low and bring the boil to a simmer. Using a slotted spoon, lower the tea bags—string and staple removed— into the liquid and let them steep for 5 to 8 minutes.

Once the saucepan is wafting warm spices your way, remove the tea bags with a slotted spoon and continue to simmer until the cranberries have just burst, about 3 minutes.

Drain the liquid and transfer the soft cranberries to a food processor or powerful blender with the orange juice and puree until smooth.

In a small bowl, whisk the remaining sugar, eggs, egg yolks and zest together.

Pour the cranberry puree through a fine mesh sieve into a clean saucepan over medium-high heat. If you want to avoid food waste, pour the cranberry puree straight into the saucepan. You'll have some cranberry skins in your pie, but they don't disrupt the taste at all.

Pour the egg mixture into the saucepan and whisk constantly, and nearly furiously, to avoid clumps of eggs until thickened, about 6 to 8 minutes.

Pour the curd into your pre-baked tart shell and let it set in the fridge for at least 2 hours before slicing in.

SPECULAAS PARSNIP TAART

My Oma used to greet me on her visits with three Dutch spice cookies bigger than my face called speculaas brokken. We'd sit in the car, sticking our hands into the package and pulling out chunks of crisp, deeply spiced spears. By the time we arrived home, half a cookie would be left and we wouldn't tell anyone. The spice is deep and snuggles into your tongue, inspiring salivation that leaves you wanting more.

PREP: 7 MINUTES / ACTIVE: 7 MINUTES / BAKING: 55–60 MINUTES / TOTAL: 1 HOUR 12 MINUTES / MAKES ONE 9" (23-CM) PIE

1½ lbs / 620 g parsnips, washed, peeled and chopped into ½" (1-cm) coins, makes about 1½ cups (360 ml) puree

¼ cup / 59 ml maple syrup

2 tbsp / 25 g granulated sugar

1 tbsp / 14 ml honey

1 tbsp + 1 tsp / 8 g Speculaas Spice (page 16)

Dash of salt

½ cup / 118 ml heavy cream

2 eggs

Speculaas cookies, crumbled, optional

Preheat the oven to 350°F (175°C).

Prepare Oma's traditional pie dough and your tin (page 25).

Transfer the parsnips to a medium saucepan and cover with water. Bring to a boil over medium-high heat and cook until they are tender, about 15 to 20 minutes. Drain the water and puree the tender parsnip coins in a food processor or powerful blender with the maple syrup until smooth. Transfer the puree to a mixing bowl.

Stir in the sugar, honey, spice and salt, followed by the heavy cream and eggs, one at a time. Pour the filling into your prepared pie shell and bake for 55 to 60 minutes.

Allow the pie to cool on a rack for at least 2 hours and top with crumbled speculaas cookies if you can find them!

DARK CHOCOLATE SPEARMINT TART

How is it that when you brush your teeth and drink orange juice, it's like an earthquake in your mouth, but when you pair chocolate with mint, the birds sing? It's something I wonder about but don't spend much time worrying over because spearmint lost in a slew of chocolate is an odd bliss for the taste buds. This rich pie has the texture of a fudge-like cake and leaves you feeling as fresh as ever thanks to the spearmint.

PREP: 5 MINUTES / ACTIVE: 9 MINUTES / BAKE: 50 MINUTES / TOTAL: 1 HOUR 4 MINUTES / MAKES ONE 8" (20-CM) TART

¼ cup / 50 g dark brown sugar

¼ cup / 50 g light brown sugar

½ cup / 120 g unbleached all-purpose flour

½ tsp salt

½ cup (1 stick) / 115 g unsalted butter

6 oz / 171 g, about 1 cup + 1 tbsp dark chocolate (67%), coarsely chopped

2 large eggs

1 tbsp / 2 g spearmint

1 peppermint stick, coarsely chopped (optional)

Preheat the oven to 350°F (175°C).

Prepare Oma's traditional pie dough and your tin (page 25).

Combine the sugars, flour and salt in a small bowl. Whisk them together until no lumps remain.

Place a heatproof bowl over a pot with an inch (2.5 cm) of boiling water. Melt the butter and then stir in the chocolate with a rubber spatula or wooden spoon. Once the chocolate is smooth and silky, transfer the bowl from the heat to a cooling rack using oven mitts to avoid any burns!

Stir the flour and sugar mixture into the chocolate a little at a time and combine until the chocolate looks sandy.

Add the eggs and spearmint, stirring until the mixture is smooth again.

Pour the filling into your prepared pie shell and bake for 50 minutes. A toothpick inserted into the center of the pie should come out close to clean. It's okay if a few crumbs remain on the toothpick!

Allow the pie to cool on a rack for at least 1 hour before enjoying with crushed peppermint on top!

BROWN BUTTER MAPLE CARROT PIE

If you get carrots from your yard, a farm or a local market, you will feel deceived by the carrots you've been served all along. Carrots are like little candy sticks that grow in the ground. And their levels of sweetness vary based on growing techniques and soil. When they're good, they're candy and don't need much more than a little maple syrup to assist in transforming the vegetable into a dessert.

This pie is similar to carrot cake. Its bite has a smooth but granular texture thanks to carrot and nut bits. The pie is thick, nutty and I think you can get away with eating it for breakfast.

PREP: 15 MINUTES / ACTIVE: 5 MINUTES / BAKING: 55-60 MINUTES / TOTAL: 1 HOUR 15-20 MINUTES / MAKES TWO 9" (23-CM) PIES

4 tbsp / 56 g unsalted butter

2 lbs / 920 g carrots, peeled and chopped into ½" (1-cm) coins

1 tsp cinnamon

¼ tsp ginger

¼ tsp cardamom

⅓ cup / 78 ml heavy cream

½ cup / 118 g maple syrup

2 tbsp / 25 g maple sugar

2 eggs

Dash of salt

¼ cup / 38 g chopped raw almonds or walnuts, optional

Preheat the oven to 350°F (175°C).

Prepare Oma's traditional pie dough and your tin (page 25).

Over medium heat, melt the butter in a medium saucepan. When it starts to hiss like an orchestra of angry rattlers, watch closely and swirl the pot around occasionally to prevent burning. The milk solids in the butter will begin to turn gold and deepen in hue. Keep cooking and swirling until the butter smells like toasted nuts and is visibly brown, 5 to 7 minutes. Pour the brown butter into a small heatproof bowl and let cool as you continue preparing the filling.

Transfer the carrot coins to a medium saucepan and cover with water. Bring the carrots to a boil and cook until tender, about 12 to 15 minutes. Drain the water from the carrots. Be careful of the steam!

In a food processor or blender, process the carrots together with the spices and brown butter until pureed and smooth. In a mixing bowl, whisk in the heavy cream, maple syrup and maple sugar, followed by the eggs, salt and almonds.

Pour the filling into your prepared pie shell and bake for 55 to 60 minutes. Allow the pie to cool for up to 1 hour before slicing in.

SALTED DATE TART

I sum up dates with the saying "looks can be deceiving." More blob of blah than vibrant fruit, the date is a tremendous sweetener that threatens sugar's place in the pantry. This tart is sweet, has no added sugar and can be devoured suddenly. It's creamy and soft, with a bite that's like butter. The texture is similar to a honey pie.

PREP: 6 MINUTES / ACTIVE: 3 MINUTES / BAKING: 50 MINUTES / TOTAL: 59 MINUTES / MAKES ONE 8" (20-CM) TART

16 dates, yields ½ cup / 118 ml date paste

½ cup / 118 ml water

2 tbsp / 29 ml heavy cream

3 tbsp / 44 ml honey

¼ cup / 55 g unsalted butter, melted

2 large eggs

1 tsp vanilla extract

½ tsp salt

½ tsp cinnamon

¼ tsp ginger

Preheat the oven to 350°F (175°C).

Prepare Oma's traditional pie dough and your tin (page 25).

To make a date paste, cover the dates with the water and microwave for 60 seconds. It's important not to cook them too long and make the dates too hot, or they'll end up too mushy to puree. You can also cover the dates with water in a mason jar and let them soak overnight. Transfer the dates and ¼ cup (59 ml) of the water to a food processor or blender and puree until you have a smooth paste, about 3 minutes.

In a large bowl, stir the heavy cream and honey into the date puree until fully incorporated.

Stir in the melted butter and then whisk in the eggs, vanilla, salt and spices until smooth.

Pour the filling into your prepared pie shell. Bake for 50 minutes. Allow the pie to cool on a rack for 2 hours to set completely.

LEMON OLIVE OIL MINI TARTS

There is an island off of Naples, Italy called Ischia and it smells like lemons—so essentially like heaven. Italians, I have experienced, know how to take a lemon and make it better. Take limoncello for example, where lemonade meets alcohol. On a warm deck overlooking the Tyrrhenian sea, a friend and I were greeted by our hosts with shots of limoncello. We sipped, enjoying the view and sharing the simple pleasures of a weekday on an Italian island with few cars in May. To me, lemons are a tango of simplicity and complexity. While refreshing, their citrus is also sour and often hard to swallow without at least one clenched eye. And by that I mean exciting. While lemons can be in season year-round, the Meyer lemon is technically a winter citrus and can be used in this recipe. These mini tartlets are for sharing and relishing.

PREP: 8 MINUTES / ACTIVE: 9 MINUTES / TOTAL: 17 MINUTES / MAKES 4 MINI TARTLETS

½ cup / 120 ml lemon juice, from 4 large lemons

Zest from 4 lemons

½ cup / 100 g sugar

3 egg yolks

2 large eggs

Pinch of salt

1 tbsp / 14 ml olive oil

2 tbsp / 29 ml limoncello liqueur

1 tsp lemon verbena, minced

Prepare Oma's traditional pie dough and blind-bake your tart tins (page 25). Because these are mini pies, blind bake for 40 minutes. Remove the tin foil and bake for 5 more minutes.

In a medium saucepan over medium-high heat, bring the lemon juice, lemon zest, sugar, egg yolks, eggs and salt to a simmer while stirring constantly with a wooden spoon. Keep stirring until the mixture is thickened, about 6 to 8 minutes, and the curd coats the back of the spoon. To know it's thick beyond this vague expression, run your finger through it (be careful, it'll be hot!) and if your finger leaves a streak, it's a good consistency.

Remove the curd from the heat and stir in the olive oil and limoncello. Fold in the minced lemon verbena.

Pour the mixture into your pre-baked tart shells and let the curd set in the fridge for at least 2 hours, or overnight, before slicing in.

CRANBERRY SAUCE APPLE PIE

The first time I experimented with a pie flavor other than apple, it was by tossing a handful of dried cranberries in with the slices. Traditionally, the appeltaart is made with raisins mixed in but my Oma stopped making it that way when my mom started picking around the raisins.

The result was a chewy, extra tart taste burrowed between the apples. It was enough of a change to spotlight the importance of said change. This pie takes it a step further by emphasizing the cranberry. Making your own cranberry sauce is so easy, it's baffling why cans of it exist. Dressing slices with the sauce almost marinates them in a dose of tart tang. It's nice to bite into something familiar but be greeted with a little something extra.

PREP: 11 MINUTES / ACTIVE: 3 MINUTES / BAKING: 45 MINUTES / TOTAL: 59 MINUTES TO 1 HOUR 4 MINUTES / MAKES ONE 10" (25-CM) PIE

8 oz (about 2 cups) / 224 g organic cranberries, washed

¼ cup / 59 ml water

¼ cup / 59 ml freshly squeezed orange juice

2 tbsp / 25 g maple sugar

2 tbsp / 29 ml maple syrup

2 lbs (about 3) / 932 g tart apples, Mutsu or Granny Smith, sliced ⅛" (3-mm) thin

Zest from 1 orange

Preheat the oven to 350°F (175°C).

Prepare Oma's traditional pie dough and your tin (page 25).

Place the cranberries in a medium saucepan over medium heat with ¼ cup (59 ml) of water, orange juice, maple sugar and maple syrup and bring to a boil. Lower the heat to a simmer and let the cranberries break and thicken, about 15 to 20 minutes. Remove the pan from the heat.

Gently lower the apples into the cranberry sauce and toss. Stir in the orange zest. Allow the filling to cool for 10 minutes and then pour into your prepared pie shell.

Bake for 45 minutes, or until crust is golden brown. Allow the pie to cool for 30 to 35 minutes before slicing in.

CHOCOLATE COCONUT TAART

There is a supposed great divide between people with a taste for pie and those who prefer cake. This is the kind of taart to patch up those cracks in dessert versus dessert. The crust of this taart gives you the crumb of a shortbread cookie, while the filling is more like a moist cake. They come together to make pie and provide peace. It's a compromise without compromising flavor, texture or taste. Dig into this rich delight to have your cake and pie too. Chocolate never goes out of a season and while the produce to bake a sweet pie might be limited during the winter, especially in New York, you can still enjoy the dessert. Coconuts are produced year-round instead of just one season, so you can find them and their shavings at any time.

PREP: 5 MINUTES / ACTIVE: 10 MINUTES / BAKING: 55-60 MINUTES / TOTAL: 1 HOUR 15 MINUTES / MAKES ONE 9" (23-CM) PIE

¼ cup / 50 g light brown sugar

¼ cup / 50 g granulated sugar

½ cup / 64 g unbleached all-purpose flour

1 tsp cinnamon

½ tsp salt

½ cup (1 stick) / 115 g unsalted butter

6 oz (about 1 cup + 1 tbsp) / 170 g bittersweet chocolate (62%), coarsely chopped

½ tsp vanilla extract

2 large eggs

½ cup / 30 g shredded coconut

Ice cream, for serving, optional

Fresh fruit, for serving, optional

Preheat the oven to 350°F (175°C).

Prepare Oma's traditional pie dough and your tin (page 25).

Combine the brown sugar, sugar, flour, cinnamon and salt in a small bowl. Whisk these ingredients together with a fork until no lumps remain. If the brown sugar insists on remaining in a lump, break it up with your fingers and mix again with your fork.

Place a small heatproof bowl over a small saucepan with an inch (2.5 cm) of boiling water. Melt the butter and then stir in the chocolate with a rubber spatula. Once the chocolate is smooth, remove the pan from heat using oven mitts to avoid getting burned.

Stir the flour and sugar mixture into the chocolate a third at a time and combine until the chocolate looks sandy.

Add the vanilla and eggs. Whisk together until the mixture is smooth again. Fold in the shredded coconut until thoroughly distributed.

Pour the filling into your prepared pie shell and bake for 55 to 60 minutes. Insert a toothpick after 45 minutes. If it comes out clean, your pie is done. It's okay for there to be a few crumbs clinging to the toothpick! Allow the pie to cool for at least 1 hour on a rack before enjoying with a scoop of ice cream and a side of fresh fruit!

SPICED FLOURLESS CHOCOLATE PIE

In my gluten-free days, I cherished flourless chocolate cakes. The little rich, fudgy saucers made life without wheat enjoyable and I confided in them. I'd purchase one with a tall glass of lemonade and the citrus zing framed the richness of the chocolate like a diploma your doctor would hang in their office. It was something to be admired up front and center. This pie is all of that. It melts in your mouth atop a crisp canvas of crust. To indulge in death by chocolate, use the chocolate pie crust here. Make it gluten-free by substituting the all-purpose flour with chickpea flour.

PREP: 6 MINUTES / ACTIVE: 20 MINUTES / TOTAL: 1 HOUR 11 MINUTES / MAKES ONE 9" (23-CM) PIE

9 oz / 255 g bittersweet chocolate, coarsely chopped

6 tbsp / 85 g unsalted butter, cut into cubes

1 tbsp / 14 ml olive oil

6 eggs, separated

¼ tsp salt

2 tsp / 10 g chili pepper, finely chopped

2 tsp / 4 g lemon zest

¾ cups / 150 g granulated sugar, divided

Preheat the oven to 350°F (175°C).

Prepare Oma's chocolate pie dough and your tin (page 25).

In a double boiler, or heatproof bowl fitted over a saucepan of boiling water about 1-inch (2.5 cm) deep, add the chocolate, butter and olive oil. Stir the ingredients together with a rubber spatula until melted and silky.

Separate the egg whites from egg yolks. Whisk the egg yolks together and add the salt, chili pepper, lemon zest and ½ cup (96 g) of sugar, stirring together until combined.

In a stand mixer, whisk the egg whites on medium-low until just frothy. As the whites continue to stiffen, gradually add the last ¼ cup (48 g) of sugar, gently sprinkling it into the whipping egg whites like winter's first snow shower. Dumping it all in at once will cause the whites to separate and give way to a grainy texture that doesn't quite work!

Add the egg yolk mixture to the chocolate and stir to combine. Fold the egg whites into the chocolate, a little at a time to maintain ultimate fluffiness.

Pour the filling into your prepared pie shell and bake for 45 minutes.

Allow the pie to cool on a rack for at least 1 hour before slicing in.

MARY LOU'S BROWN SUGAR ALMOND PIE

My grandmother on my father's side claims that she is a "mixed bag of nuts." She's a jolly woman from Virginia whose belly bounces when she laughs, which is often. We spend most mornings in the kitchen sipping coffee together and waiting for Poppie to be done scrambling eggs so that we can dig in. She's cooked for me since always and has taught me the cheesy lessons of building a mac & cheese casserole. This is the only pie we've ever baked together. It can be baked any time of the year, but because of its richness, it's best enjoyed in the winter months when you need a little "extra padding" to keep warm.

PREP: 2 MINUTES / ACTIVE: 1 MINUTE / BAKING: 45–50 MINUTES / TOTAL: 53 MINUTES / MAKES ONE 9" (23-CM) PIE

3 eggs

½ cup / 100 g light brown sugar

¼ cup / 50 g dark brown sugar

½ cup / 118 ml honey

¼ cup / 55 g butter, melted

1 cup / 140 g raw almonds, coarsely chopped

Preheat the oven to 350°F (175°C).

Prepare Oma's traditional pie dough and your tin (page 25).

Beat the eggs and then whisk in both the sugars, honey and melted butter. Stir in the almonds and pour into your prepared pie shell.

Bake for 45 to 50 minutes until the center is just about set. It should jiggle in the middle as you take it out of the oven. Allow the pie to cool on a rack for at least 2 hours to fully set before slicing in.

SPICED GRAPEFRUIT CURD TART

The only way I've ever enjoyed grapefruit was with a mound of sugar on top. That is obviously very unhealthy and defeats the purpose of eating a grapefruit for breakfast in the first place. But tarts allow sugar and a heaping of spices to cure the inherent bitterness that shrivels up some people's tongues. The grapefruit flavor here offers that winter citrus and all the good tang. But the sugar and spices play along to not let too much tang take the spotlight.

PREP: 8 MINUTES / ACTIVE: 15 MINUTES / TOTAL: 23 MINUTES / YIELDS 1½ CUPS (354 ML) CURD / MAKES ONE 9"(23-CM) TART

3 eggs

2 egg yolks

¾ cups / 150 g sugar

½ tsp freshly grated ginger

1 tsp cardamom

¼ tsp cinnamon

¼ tsp nutmeg

¼ tsp kosher salt

1 tbsp / 6 g grapefruit zest

½ tbsp / 3 g blood orange zest

2 large grapefruits, makes about ¾ cups / 177 ml grapefruit juice

¼ cup / 59 ml blood orange juice

4 tbsp / 56 g unsalted butter

1 tsp vanilla extract

Prepare Oma's traditional pie dough and pre-bake the dough (page 25).

Beat the eggs and egg yolks together with sugar, ginger, spices, salt and zests with a whisk. Combine the mixture with the grapefruit juice and blood orange juice in a medium saucepan over medium-high heat and stir constantly with a wooden spoon until the mixture has thickened, about 10 to 15 minutes. You'll know your curd is thick enough when it coats the back of the wooden spoon. If you run your finger through it (careful, it will be hot!), it should leave a streak. Stir in the butter and vanilla for a silky-smooth texture that glistens under the kitchen lights.

Pour the curd into your pre-baked tart shell and let it set in the fridge for at least 2 hours, or up to overnight, before slicing in.

NOTE: If you can't find blood oranges, using a naval orange is fine!

EGG-FREE ROSEMARY CHOCOLATE SILK PIE

This is a no-bake filling that sits plush like a cloud in crust. Instead of using eggs in the silk pie, which would then be consumed raw, this pie expands by way of aquafaba. Meaning, this pie uses the thick liquid found in a can of garbanzo beans. The chickpea water has gained traction in vegan baking for its ability to mock the characteristics of an egg. If this sounds off putting to you, don't fear. The chocolate does not fall prey to the taste of chickpeas. Instead, what you get is a pudding-like filling that's safe for everyone to eat and that is easily licked off the spoon (or fork, however you decide to devour it).

PREP: 5 MINUTES / ACTIVE: 5 MINUTES / TOTAL: 18 MINUTES / MAKES ONE 9" (23-CM) PIE

4 oz / 113 g bittersweet chocolate (58–60%)

1 cup (2 sticks) / 226 g unsalted butter, softened

1 cup / 100 g granulated sugar

Sprinkle of sea salt

1 tsp vanilla extract

⅓ cup / 78 ml aquafaba, from one can of garbanzo beans

1 tbsp / 15 ml rosemary, coarsely chopped

TIPS: To make this pie vegan, make sure to get vegan chocolate and use vegan butter!

If you do not own a stand mixer or hand mixer, I have witnessed my friend passionately beating softened butter and sugar together to achieve this consistency with the force of her biceps and whisk. She broke a sweat, and labored over the ingredients for much longer than 2 minutes, but ultimately succeeded.

Prepare Oma's traditional pie dough and blind-bake your crust (page 25).

In a heatproof bowl set over a pot of boiling water, melt the chocolate. Remove from the heat using oven mitts to prevent burning your fingers! Allow the chocolate to cool thoroughly.

Fit a stand mixer with the paddle attachment and combine the butter, sugar and salt together in its bowl. Beat until the butter and sugar have become a light and creamy mixture of heaven, about 2 minutes on medium speed. Make sure to scrape the butter back into the bowl.

With the mixer still running on medium speed, pour in the melted and cooled chocolate. Continue to mix until the chocolate is one with the butter. Scrape any chocolate-butter from the sides of the bowl back into the center. With a rubber spatula, make sure to remove all the chocolate butter from the paddle attachment before fitting the mixer with the whisk.

On a low speed, begin to whisk in the vanilla. Pour the aquafaba in a little at a time with the whisk running on medium speed. Allow the whisk to whip it into the chocolate for 2 minutes before pouring more. The filling will begin to form soft peaks and grow in volume. Continue until all the aquafaba has been used, about 6 minutes, making sure to stop the motor and scrape the chocolate on the sides of the bowl back in for an even whip. Fold in the rosemary.

Pour the fluffy filling into your pre-baked pie crust and enjoy immediately!

HONEY SWEET POTATO PIE

Squash is wonderful, but it isn't the only vegetable that gets to have fun. Sweet potatoes are resilient and know no season. They're always abundant and maybe CSA members are tired of them come March, but despite exhausting uses for them, they remain a staple past Thanksgiving.

PREP: 18 MINUTES / ACTIVE: 3 MINUTES / BAKING: 60–65 MINUTES / TOTAL: 2 HOURS 6 MINUTES / MAKES TWO 9" (23-CM) PIES

*2 large sweet potatoes, peeled, makes
1½ cups / 360 ml puree*

¼ cup / 59 ml honey

½ cup / 100 g light brown sugar

½ tsp cinnamon

¼ tsp ginger

¼ tsp ground cloves

¼ tsp cardamom

¼ tsp nutmeg

Dash of salt

¾ cup / 177 ml heavy cream

2 eggs

1 tsp vanilla extract

Preheat the oven to 350°F (175°C).

Prepare Oma's traditional pie dough and your tin (page 25).

Wrap the sweet potatoes in tin foil and roast whole on a baking sheet for 45 to 55 minutes until they can be easily pierced with a fork.

Once the potatoes have cooled enough to handle, peel the skin off and puree the meat in a food processor or powerful blender until smooth, about 4 to 5 minutes.

In a bowl, whisk the honey and light brown sugar into the sweet potato puree. Mix in the spices and salt. Slowly pour in the heavy cream and whisk together until the potato puree is a light orange. Add the eggs one at a time, followed by the vanilla, and whisk until thoroughly combined.

Pour the filling into your prepared pie shell and bake for 60 to 65 minutes, or until golden brown. Allow the pie to cool on a rack for at least 1 hour before slicing in.

ACKNOWLEDGMENTS

Thank you to my family—the Bennetts, the Warshaws, the Vogels, the Vles, the Schensemas, and the Sterns. Without your unwavering support and taste testing abilities, this book would not have been written. Your love and spontaneous kitchen dance breaks have been a surge of positivity in my life. I am so lucky to learn from you all.

An immense gratitude is owed to my best friends—Kaitlyn, Rebecca S., Bettina, Rebecca B. and Nick—for constantly being armed with a fork in hand to taste test. I am in awe of your pie eating abilities and your deep kindness. Thank you for lending honest feedback and always, always being there.

This book would be impossible without the first pie, which appeared and kept appearing in the Bruno family kitchen Thanksgiving after Thanksgiving. Thank you for believing in Taartwork and always having an appeltaart on your table. I could not be more grateful.

Thank you to Morgan without whom these pies wouldn't have a spotlight. Thank you for coming to my kitchen all those years ago to capture the first few taarts and for sticking around to capture these new creations. Your eye for detail is inspiring and I'm so lucky to have had you by my side during this creative process. Thank you to Kat for providing your design talent.

These pies would not be possible without the produce from the small and local farmers in New York and Pennsylvania. Thank you to Roxbury Farm, Taproot Farm and Sweet Earth Company. The vegetables, fruit and flowers grown from your soil have made what I bake taste immensely better. You did all the hard work; I'm just slicing and dicing. Thank you to Local Roots NYC without whom I would not have such a connection to this produce. And thank you to my friends at Churncraft for teaching me how to churn my own butter.

I am eternally grateful to the Spannocchia Foundation in Italy. An internship program radically altered the way I conduct my business and live my life. Thank you for introducing me to a community of inspiring people. Thank you to Maddy, Jillian, Olivia, Josh, Delfina, Sarah, Anxo, Andres and Nate for always being in the kitchen cooking something. Thank you to Yago for always reminding us to proceed "with calm."

And finally, thank you to my Oma Margaretha, to whom this book is dedicated, for keeping me healthy and loving your entire family fiercely and so selflessly. You are everything I admire.

ABOUT THE AUTHOR

Brittany Bennett is a writer and baker rooted in Brooklyn, NY. Her writing has appeared on NYLON.com and The Coveteur. After a stint in the Los Angeles media industry, she returned to New York and whipped up Taartwork in 2015. Learning from her Oma's grace in the kitchen, Brittany remixed the original Dutch apple recipe to include more seasonal produce and fit into a typical American pie dish. Her pies have appeared in *Vogue*, Vogue.com, *Bustle* and *W* magazine.

INDEX

N

O

P